WHERE'S TH

Preparing and Producing the Software User's Manual

Richard A. McGrath

VNR VAN NOSTRAND REINHOLD
New York

Copyright © 1991 by Van Nostrand Reinhold

Library of Congress Catalog Number 90-41439
ISBN 0-442-00425-7

Previously published and copyrighted as Consultant's Reports CR–34 and CR–34s, by Richard A. McGrath and Studio 7 Technical Documentation, 2640 Melendy Drive, San Carlos, CA 94070.

Printed in the United States of America

Van Nostrand Reinhold
115 Fifth Avenue
New York, New York 10003

Chapman and Hall
2-6 Boundary Row
London SE1 8HN, England

Thomas Nelson Australia
102 Dodds Sreet
South Melbourne 3205, Victoria, Australia

Nelson Canada
1120 Birchmont Road
Scarborough, Ontario M1K 5G4, Canada

16 15 14 13 12 11 10 9 8 7 6 5 4 3 2 1

Library of Congress Cataloging-in-Publication Data

McGrath, Richard A.
        Where's the manual? preparing and producing the software user's
    manual / Richard A. McGrath
            p.   cm.
        Includes index.
         ISBN 0-442-00425-7
        1. Computer software--Handbooks, manuals, etc. 2. Software
    documentation. I. Title. II. Title: Where is the manual.
    QA76.755.M38 1991
    005.1'5--dc20   90-41439
                                                        CIP

Table of Contents

Illustrations

Preface

Excellent software user's manuals exist, but they are atypical. If you read computer magazines or talk to people who use today's programs, an industry-wide agreement surfaces. Whether the programs are written for use on mainframes or microcomputers, both novices and professionals say: "The user's manuals are terrible." How has this come about? The answer is: lack of planning.

Ideally, a user's manual should be written before the programmers develop the software because software specifications are a natural extension of the functional description spelled out in the user's manual.

Often, however, the sequence of events during software development is not ideal. Software is frequently written with very little attention to the user's need for written instructions. Then, at the last minute, someone says, "Where's the manual?" The kind of documentation that results stems from a rush to meet marketing deadlines and an eleventh-hour production run. Both of these symptoms are evidence of poor planning.

You may think that this sort of thing happens only in start-up companies. It isn't true. In Fortune 500 businesses, the lack of planning simply takes another form. The most carefully devised plan is cast aside when a manager says, at the last minute, "We have to include this new feature." The problem here is failure to recognize the importance of a freeze date. The ripple-effect of adding the new feature produces a result not unlike the lack of planning in many start-up companies.

About the Book and the Audience

Where's the Manual? has two parts. Part I contains sections on planning, organizing, scheduling, writing, and producing a ready-to-print manual. The approach is a a practical one: Text is prepared on a word processor and illustrations are done by hand or with a computer-aided design package such as AutoCAD. Words and pictures are then combined by the classical cut-and-paste methods. If you're on a limited budget, this approach ensures that you'll produce a cost-effective manual. In Part I, we assume that you'll use a word processor, cut-and-paste technology, and not much desktop publishing at all.

Part II (Chapters 5 through 7) describes desktop publishing on an IBM XT/AT or 386 platform, using Xerox's Ventura Publisher software. Why did we do this? Most books in this field focus on desktop publishing and assume that the classical business of waxing galleys and positioning halftones on pasteup boards is something from distant history.

I have operated a technical writing, graphics and consulting business for about 10 years in a period that coincides with the desktop publishing revolution. We have a desktop publishing system like the one described in this book, but not everyone in the world is as committed to desktop publishing with the fervor that magazines and equipment manufacturers would like you to have.

Many companies operate on a philosophy of "If it ain't broke, don't fix it." In the world of technical manuals, this translates into: "What we've been doing for the last five years still works, so why do we need all this fancy equipment?" There are managers who will spend money on engineering workstations and computer-driven milling machines, but why would they want to waste their budget on equipment and software just to prepare manuals? "Look," they say, "that's what the technical writers are paid to do."

Then, there are the start-up companies. The bright people in these companies have heard about desktop publishing and they want some. When they find that it costs money, they decide they don't want any at all. Then, in the staff meeting, they reach a compromise that goes something like this: "Harry's secretary is great at word processing. We'll buy a laser printer and let her do the manuals."

Desktop (or "electronic") publishing is displacing classical cut-and-paste technology in the small business and corporate setting. As a result, a bridge is needed between the classical cut-and-paste technology and desktop publishing. This is not a book that details all the ins and outs of electronic publishing. Many other people have published on this topic so we decided not to reproduce their efforts. This is not a book or report that compares desktop publishing on the Macintosh, the Sun, and the PC/XT/AT, nor is it a primer on technical writing and page composition. Many books, reports, periodicals, and newsletters discuss these things and some of these publications are listed under Selected Readings.

This book is for people like Harry's secretary, or the bright people in start-up companies, or the cost-conscious managers who see documentation as a necessary evil. The memo that comes around might read something like this:

• Produce a manual.
• Use existing equipment and software.
• Only buy what you need.

The camera-ready masters for *Where's the Manual?* were prepared by a combination of electronic publishing and classical cut-and-paste techniques. Although there are people who think this is "cheating," the approach is a practical alternative to cluttering one's hard disk and slowing a small system with a large number of picture files.

How the Book Is Organized

Part I   Working without Desktop Publishing Tools

Chapter 1. "Planning, Organizing, and Scheduling" is a roadmap. The necessary software and hardware tools are considered. Research requirements and outlining are covered. Planning for contract services and reviews, scheduling of time and costs, and the importance of a freeze date are discussed.

Chapter 2. "Writing the Main Sections" contains instructions, examples, and guidelines for writing and illustrating the main sections of the user's manual. The main sections are the Introduction, Ground Rules and Procedures, and Step-by-Step Instructions.

Chapter 3. "Writing the Back Matter and Front Matter" covers the structure and format of the supplementary material at the end of the user's manual: the Reference Guide, Error Codes, Appendices, Glossary, Index, and Readers' Response Card. The Front Matter, the material at the beginning of the manual, is discussed, with special attention given to developing an accurate Table of Contents and List of Figures, which can only be done after the Back Matter is finished.

Chapter 4. "Production "describes the use of computer-aided tools and techniques for transforming text and rough sketches into camera-ready master copy for the printer. Conventional typesetting, "Typewriter Manuals," and laser-based typography are compared as production styles. Mounting of graphics, formatting text, and paste-up procedures are described.

Part II Working with Desktop Publishing Tools

Chapter 5: "About Electronic Publishing" describes the origin of desktop publishing and answers common questions about this art and craft.

Chapter 6: "The PC Approach "describes the required tools based on MS-DOS or PC-DOS software together with hardware for IBM PC/XT/AT and Compaq 386 computers. Most of the material in this section can also be applied to IBM's OS/2 and PS/2 family and to various PC clones.

Chapter 7: "Special Ventura Applications" describes what can be done with this new generation of tools. This chapter is designed for someone who already knows how to use Xerox's Ventura Publisher. In this chapter, you'll find a collection of tips and tricks for getting the most out of your PC-based desktop publishing system plus a crash course in typography. Two applications are discussed in detail: capturing and incorporating screen images into a document and use of the scanner as a desktop publishing tool.

Back Matter: At the back of the book are several short sections: Two Appendices, a Glossary, Selected Readings, and an Index.

Acknowledgments

Many thanks to my parents, Roy and Gertrude McGrath for their ongoing encouragement of this project, to Sandra Mariner for her comments during preparation of the original manuscript, to Vince Swanson for his insights into Macintosh systems, and to Dianne Littwin, Senior Editor at Van Nostrand Reinhold, for a thousand helpful suggestions.

The following registered trademarks and tradenames are cited in *Where's the Manual?*

Above Board	Intel, Inc.
Adobe Illustrator	Adobe Systems, Inc.
AT&T 6300	American Telephone and Telegraph
AutoCAD	Autodesk, Inc.
Brief	UnderWare, Inc.
Byte	McGraw-Hill, Inc.
Canon IX-12	Canon (U.S.A.), Inc.
CHART	Microsoft Corp.
Compaq	Compaq Computer Corp.
Computer Graphics World	Pennwell Publishing Co.
Cricket Draw	Cricket Software
Crosstalk	Microstuf, Inc.
Designer	Micrografx, Inc.
Diablo 620, 630	Diablo Systems, Inc.

Displaywrite	International Business Machines, Inc.
DMP-51, DMP-61	Houston Instrument Co.
Dr. Halo	Media Cybernetics, Inc.
EasyCad	Evolution Computing
Epson	Epson America, Inc.
FastCad	Evolution Computing
Fontware	Bitstream, Inc.
GEM	Digital Research, Inc.
GRAFTALK	The Redding Group
GRAMMATIK	Digital Marketing Corp.
Graphics Master	Tecmar, Inc.
Grubblie	Studio 7 Technical Documentation
Harvard Business Graphics	Software Publishing Co.
Hayes	Hayes Microcomputer Products, Inc.
Helvetica, Times	Linotype AG
Hercules	Hercules Computer Technology, Inc.
HI	Houston Instrument Co.
HOTSHOT	Symsoft, Inc.
H-P, HPGL, 7475	Hewlett-Packard Co.
IBM	International Business Machines, Inc.
Illustrator	Adobe Systems, Inc.
INDEX	Digital Marketing Corp.
Interleaf Publisher	Interleaf, Inc.
J-Laser, J-Laser Plus	TallTree Systems, Inc.
Kiss	QMS Corp.
Koh-I-Noor	Koh-I-Noor Rapidograph, Inc.
KROY	Kroy Co.
LaserJet, LaserJet Plus	Hewlett-Packard Corp.
LaserView	Sigma Designs, Inc.
LaserWriter	Apple Computer, Inc.
Linotronic	Linotype AG
Logitech	Logitech, Inc.
Lotus 1-2-3	Lotus Development Corp.
Macintosh, Macpaint	Apple Computer, Inc.
Manuscript	Lotus Development Corp.
Mars	Staedtler Corp. (Germany)
Mentor Graphics	Mentor Graphics, Inc.
MILESTONE	Digital Marketing Corp.
Mouse Systems Mouse	Mouse Systems, Inc.
MS-DOS	Microsoft Corp.
Multimate	Ashton-Tate, Inc.
MX-100	Epson America, Inc.

NEC	NEC Home Electronics (U.S.A.), Inc.
NewGen,Turbo PS	NewGen Systems Corp.
NOVA(S)	Computrade, Inc.
PageMaker	Aldus Corp.
Pasteze	T & J Graphic Art Supplies
PC Mouse	Mouse Systems, Inc.
PC-Paintbrush	Z-Soft Corp.
PC World	PCW Communications, Inc.
Perfect Writer	Perfect Software, Inc.
Personal Publishing	Hitchcock Publishing Co.
Photo Mount	Minnesota Mining and Manufacturing Co.
Photon MEGA	Personal Computer Graphics Corp.
PostScript	Adobe Systems, Inc.
Printware, 720 IQ	Printware, Inc.
ProComm	Datastorm Technologies, Inc.
Prodesign II	American Small Business Computers, Inc.
Publish!	PCW Communications, Inc.
QMS	QMS Corp.
Ready	Living Videotext, Inc.
ScanCAD	Houston Instrument Co.
SCANGRAB	White Sciences, Inc.
Sigma Plot	Jandel Scientific
Smartmodem	Hayes Microcomputer Products, Inc.
SPELL	Software Toolworks, Inc.
STC	Society for Technical Communication
Tech-Graph-Pad	Binary Engineering Software, Inc.
THE WORD PLUS	Oasis Systems, Inc.
TYP-SET	Enter Computer Co.
Ventura Publisher	Xerox Corp.
VersaCad	VersaCAD Corp.
VP-to-the-Max	Aristocad, Inc.
WORD	Microsoft Corp.
Word Perfect	Word Perfect Corp.
WordStar	MicroPro International Corp.
Xerox Writer	Xerox Corp.

Part I

Working without Desktop Publishing Tools

1

Planning, Organizing, and Scheduling

Chapter 1 covers tools needed, research requirements, outlining, planning, and scheduling. Allow a minimum of two to four weeks to complete these steps.

COLLECT YOUR TOOLS

The "Tools" section describes the hardware and needed to produce a professional user's manual. Later on, this book will discuss true desktop publishing systems that might make many of the concepts described here obsolete. It is useful, however, to know how to produce a manual without specialized hardware and software. In many cases, you can substitute items for those specified. This book assumes that you will be using a mixture of what is already on hand and a few new, but necessary, items.

A Separate Word Processor

For your writing, plan to use a word processor or a microcomputer with word processing software. Do not try to run the program that you are writing about on the same machine that you are using as a writing instrument. Using two systems saves time because it enables you to check something in your program without interrupting the writing process.

Regardless of the equipment you use, your word processor should be able to generate ASCII files so that the output can be transferred to other systems. As an alternative, use a conversion utility to make the ASCII files. Usually, an IBM work-alike computer is a good choice for a writing instrument. A hard disk will speed things up because it eliminates the need for disk swapping. Look for an XT or AT clone. If you find a used IBM or Compaq machine, so much the better.

Word Processing Software

There is no ideal word processing software. Every program has good features as well as a few idiosyncracies. The necessary features are compatibility with other hardware and software, ease of use, and a What-You-See-Is-What-You-Get (WYSIWYG) display.

Excellent word processing programs are WordStar 3.0, WordStar 2000, Word Perfect, and Microsoft's WORD. With the exception of the older version of WordStar, these programs have drivers for laser-based printers. If you already have WordStar 3.0, you can transfer data files into one of the other programs to gain more versatile formatting and type style options.

Spelling, Grammar, and Indexing Software

Several secondary programs can make development of a document an easier task. SPELL (Software Toolworks) is inexpensive and compatible with several word processing programs. THE WORD PLUS (Oasis Systems) is a versatile and faster spelling package. GRAMMATIK (Digital Marketing) checks grammar and punctuation. INDEX (Digital Marketing) creates an Index and Table of Contents when used with WordStar files. If you use newer word processing software, the spelling checker and indexing options are probably built into the program.

Scheduling Software

Specialized programs are available for producing Gantt, PERT, or critical path schedules. MILESTONE (Digital Marketing) is especially suited for document production schedules. The program generates a critical path schedule and also builds a summary report that breaks down labor and fixed costs for any project of reasonable size. Output to dot-matrix, laser, or daisy-wheel printers provides hardcopy without a plotter. Better known manufacturers, such as Microsoft, also produce scheduling software. Look in stores that sell computer software for a program that suits your particular needs.

Printers

For preparing letters, documents, or drafts of manuals, use a letter-quality printer. Daisy-wheel machines, such as the Diablo 620 or 630, are excellent choices and provide several type styles that should suit most applications. Currently, letter-quality printers cost from $200 (at discount) to about $1,700. A near-letter-quality dot-matrix printer is not a suitable alternative because the dot-matrix image becomes fuzzy when reproduced. If you can afford an in-house laser printing engine, the Hewlett-Packard LaserJet or Apple's less expensive LaserWriter are ideal for preparing camera-ready text that has a near-typeset look.

Graphics Hardware

Line drawings can be generated by an illustrator with drafting pens, a T-square, and drawing board—or with computer-aided design (CAD) software and a quality plotter. The most popular and versatile plotters are Hewlett-Packard's 7475A and Houston Instrument's DMP-61. Both plotters produce drawings at a resolution of 0.001". The H-P machine has a six-pen carousel and handles ANSI A/B size drawings. The DMP-61 is a single-pen plotter that manages A- to D- size output; a 15-pen version (DMP-61 MP) is also available.

Graphics Software

For producing computer-generated line drawings, AutoCAD software (AutoDesk) is a wonderful micro-based CAD program for general-purpose applications. Use AutoCAD if you can justify the price (over $2,000) for other applications in your business. If you need only an occasional drawing, use AutoSketch (a miniversion of AutoCAD) or Prodesign II (American Small Business Computers) which can do the job for much less money. For large headings, consider Enter Computer's TYP-SET program, which produces large characters that can be plotted.

For plotting business graphics, specialized programs are faster and easier to use than drafting software. One such program is Microsoft's CHART, which produces pie, bar, or point graphs and generates legends, titles, and scales automatically.

RESEARCH REQUIREMENTS

The first objective is to determine how your program is special and what distinguishes your software from everything else on the market. With this information you can write a user's manual that emphasizes your software's strongest points.

Do Your Homework

It is important to know about programs that are similar to yours. The information is easy to find. Study trade magazines and software publications. Read review articles and everything else that you can find about similar products, your prospective users, and your competition. Collect data sheets, advertising brochures, and pamphlets that describe your competitors' products. Buying your competitors' software may be the easiest way to obtain comparable user's manuals.

Use your company's library as a source of information. The public library and bookshelves at computer stores can be valuable sources also. If your company has an advertising agency, the agency may have access to market surveys and comparisons of look-alike products.

What Are the Preconceptions?

If your company plans to market your software package, there may be an in-house style guide that you can use as a writing aid. Certain company policies (or your manual being part of a series with preestablished formats) may influence your manual's style or appearance, so know what guidelines exist before you start. If you are writing a user's manual for software that will be sent to a publisher or software distribution house, call and ask for a style guide.

Build a Special Features List

Be sure that you understand your entire program. Talk to everyone who has a part in the design of the software and ask questions. Find out which three features of the program each person considers to be the most important.

Now that you have some information, you will be able to make comparisons. Prepare a list of program features. Next to each entry, note whether your competition has that attribute. This is the first version of a special features list.

Have your Product Manager or Advertising Manager check your list and ask for suggestions and additions. Prioritize your list. At the top, list the most important special features and, at the bottom, the "me-too" items. When your features list is finished, you will be ready to start an outline.

MAKE AN OUTLINE

Writing with an outline is like driving with a map to show you where you are going. Several computer-based outlining programs are available: WORD has the outlining feature built into its word processing program; Ready (Living Videotext, Inc.) is an example of a stand-alone outline processor. If you do not have outlining software, you can do the job with any word processor by following the procedures and examples in this section.

Organize Your Thinking

An outline is an organizational tool for your thinking. If you prefer a prose version of the outline (often called a Publications Plan), follow the same procedures, but organize each topic into sentences and paragraphs instead of entering brief items. Here are the three parts of a user's manual and an example of a preliminary outline.

- The first set of elements is the Front Matter: Title Page, Acknowledgments, Copyright Notice, License Agreement and Disclaimer, Table of Contents, and List of Figures.

- Three main sections make up the body of the user's manual; the Introduction, Ground Rules and Procedures, and Step-by-Step Instructions.

- The Back Matter is a collection of material that appears at the end of the manual: the Reference Guide, Error Codes, Appendices, Glossary, Index, and Reader's Response Card.

EXAMPLE OF PRELIMINARY OUTLINE

Section I.   Front Matter
Section II.   Introduction
Section III. Ground Rules and Procedures
Section IV.   Step-by-Step Instructions
Section V.   Back Matter

Outline the Main Sections First

Consider the three main sections of your user's manual: the Introduction, Ground Rules and Procedures, and Step-by-Step Instructions. To begin your outline, write a short phrase that describes some important aspect or topic of your user's manual. (Punctuation and grammar are not important at this stage). List the phrase under one of the three main sections. Repeat the procedure: write a short phrase about another important topic and put it under a main section. Continue this process, adding each topic, feature, or activity under the appropriate main section and soon, you will have a list under each section heading.

Prioritize the topics within each main section. Decide which ideas are more important than the others and rearrange the topics in descending order of importance. As you assign priorities, refer to the list of special features that you have prepared, keeping in mind the logical sequence of events that might confront a new user of your program.

Expand the Outline

Review your preliminary outline. Group together ideas and operations that logically belong together. Within each main section, you will need to distinguish between ideas that are more important and those that are less important. Place the more important ideas in sections and the less important ones in subsections. To indicate the difference, indent the subsections and use different labeling. For example, if the sections are numbered, use letters for the subsections.

For the time being, carry miscellaneous topics (i.e., ideas that do not fit anywhere else) under a heading called "Other." The "Other" category can appear in any or all of the three main sections. Do not be overly concerned with the structure of the outline. The important thing is to get the information organized.

Outline the Front Matter and Back Matter

During the early outlining stages, keep the details to a minimum. There are at least six items required in the Front Matter:

- Title Page
- Copyright Notice
- Acknowledgments
- License Agreement and Disclaimer
- Table of Contents
- List of Figures

Back Matter typically includes the following:

- Reference Guide
- Error Codes
- Appendices
- Glossary
- Index
- Readers' Response Card

Consider the Figures

Arrange for breaks in solid blocks of text. One approach is to organize the text in an interesting pattern. Another technique is to use pictures. Graphics can convey a lot of information in a small space. A flowchart, for example, tells its story better than a long, wordy description. A photograph is an even easier way to focus your reader's attention.

Where Are Figures Needed?

The outline is your primary design tool for the user's manual. Review your outline and mark the places where figures are required. For example, under the heading "Disks and Disk Handling," you would probably include a line drawing of a disk and its parts and in the installation instructions, a figure showing the START-UP MENU would be helpful. The number of figures that you include will depend upon your program's requirements.

A Few Cartoons Can Help

One trick that can add interest to a manual is the inclusion of cartoons. Cartoons are simple to draw and a few are usually enough. During the design stages, sketches should suffice. Figure 1–1 shows an example of a cartoon character named Grubblie.

Figure 1–1. Grubblie, an easy-to-draw cartoon character.

Sample Outline

The following is an outline of the user's manual for ABC software. Notice how the figures are indicated. Intricate details have not been filled in, but there is enough information to provide an accurate idea of the manual's content. Later, this outline will be used as an example for further discussion. See Chapters 2 and 3.

USER'S MANUAL FOR ABC SOFTWARE

Section I.   Front Matter

> A. Title Page
> B. Copyright Notice
> C. Acknowledgments
> D. License Agreement and Disclaimer

Figure 0-0 (License Agreement card)

> E. Table of Contents
> F. List of Figures

Section II.   Introduction

> A. About the Program
>   1. Who is the user?
>   2. What is ABC?
>   3. Where is ABC software compatible?
>   4. When is ABC most useful?
>   5. Why is ABC necessary?
>   6. How is ABC different?
> B. System Requirements
>   1. Overview
>   2. Operating system
>   3. Memory
>   4. Disk drives
>   5. Program installation (Overview)
>   6. Compatible computers
>   7. Compatible graphics adapter cards
>   8. Compatible printers
>   9. Compatible plotters
>   10. Options
>   11. Other specifications

Secction III. Ground Rules and Procedures

    A. Disks and Disk Handling
       1. Overview
       2. Standard caution symbols
       3. Size, capacity, and density

Figure 0-0 (Line drawing—disk parts)

       4. Power ON . . . Power OFF
       5. Definitions
    B. Conventions
       1. Overview
       2. Special names and symbols
       3. Equipment instruction example
       4. Key commands
       5. Filenames

Figure 0-0 (CTRL and ESC key commands)

       6. Keyboard instruction example
       7. Screen representation
          a) Cursors and cursor movement
          b) Scrolling and panning

Figure 0-0 (Display example—full screen)
Figure 0-0 (Display example—half screen)

Section IV. Step-by-Step Instructions

    A. Overview
    B. Make Two Backup Disks
       1. Overview
       2. Step-by-step instructions
    C. Start-up Instructions
       1. Overview
       2. Step-by-step instructions

Figure 0-0 (Disk directory)
Figure 0-0 (Copyright screen)
Figure 0-0 (Start-up menu)

    D. Configuring for a Graphics Adapter Card
       1. Overview
       2. Step-by-step instructions

Figure 0-0 (Adapter card selection menu)

    E. Configuring for Input Devices
       1. Overview

        3.   Recovery Action List
    C. Appendices

1.	Appendix I	Revision Summary by Date
2.	Appendix II	Configuring Adapter Cards
3.	Appendix III	Configuring Printers
4.	Appendix IV	Configuring Plotters
5.	Appendix V	Configuring Digitizers
6.	Appendix VI	Changing of Defaults
7.	Appendix VII	Compatible Computers
8.	Appendix VIII	ASCII Codes

    D. Glossary
    E. Index
    F. Reader's Response Card

Figure 0-0 (Readers' Response card)

Perfect Your Outline

Within each category, every major heading should have at least two minor headings under it. Create new headings as needed and find a place for the "Other" entries. Select two in-house reviewers to look at your outline and ask for their comments. Incorporate the reviewers comments and suggestions into your outline.

PLAN FOR HELPERS AND SERVICES

So far, we have considered research, tools, outlining and illustrations (figures). Now we will consider who will do the work. Can you do the job alone? If you are multitalented, you may be able to handle the writing, illustrations, and everything else. Most of us, however, need all the help that we can get. How do you find the additional services and support that you will need?

Contract Writers and Others

Your company may have a drafting department. If manuals are produced in-house, technical illustrators or an advertising department may provide the help you will need for producing artwork. If your company employs people to do word processing, you might have on-board help for preparing your final draft. If you do not have in-house help available, however, what can you do? Look in the telephone book under "Temporary Help." In large cities you will find a number of job-shops that provide professional help for technical writing, word processing, illustrating, and pasteup on a contractual basis. Use your telephone to discover who is available and what these services will cost.

Professional Documentation Services

In locales that have a well-developed computer and electronics industry, you can usually find a technical documentation business or specialist who can produce a finished manual using your outline, engineering notes, and a disk copy of the program. Obtain estimates to compare the costs with your own analysis.

It is important to know how your project can be completed if key people leave your company or if it seems that the project might overrun a deadline. Some documentation companies provide a variety of services in addition to writing and illustrating, such as foreign language translation, typesetting, print-related activities, and consulting services.

Consultants: When You Need One

If you have a small budget you may not be able to afford a consultant (fees can be $100 per hour or more), but if you need to produce several user's manuals (e.g., for an entire product line), a consultant might be a valuable asset. Usually a consultant will not do the work for you but will tell you what needs to be done, where to find help, and how to get your job done on time. Consultants can be seen as synthesizers—people who can make all of the bits and pieces fit together properly because that is their special strength.

How to Get What You Pay For

When hiring a technical writer, technical illustrator, photographer, or consultant, a written contract is necessary unless you know the individual personally and have conducted business satisfactorily with that person previously. There are four topics that the written contract should cover:

- Responsible parties
- Work to be done
- Delivery schedule
- Payment schedule

Most contractors insist on an advance payment in order to start a job. Check the contractor's references before you sign on the dotted line. If the references are good, go ahead—if not, find another contractor. In any event, your attorney or legal department should approve the final contract.

Buy or Build Special Services

Some services might require equipment that is beyond your budget. For example, if you need a laser printing engine to produce camera-ready text and your budget can not support its purchase, contact a service company. Here are examples of some available services:

- Laser typography from WordStar text files
- Computer plots from sketches
- High-resolution 35mm slides from Lotus 1-2-3 files
- Translation and typesetting in foreign languages

Usually it is more cost-effective to contract for services that require expensive hardware or software than to develop a specialized facility at your expense, however, the buy-or-build decisions are complex. Shop around and also seek advice from within your company.

PLAN A TEST

After the manual has been written and all the figures have been drawn, the document has to be checked. Plan early for the final testing of your manual and allow at least 10 days to complete this process.

Test Your Manual

Somebody who is unfamiliar with your program should run the software, using the preliminary manual as a guide. In many cases, the front-office secretary may be the appropriate person to perform such an evaluation and provide comments.

If you have doubts about the test comments after the testing is finished, find a second test person and repeat the testing process. It might seem that you are starting again, but it is better to spend more time at this stage than to receive letters from irate customers. What you are insuring is a user-friendly and accurate manual.

Professional Reviewers

If you want the fastest test response possible, hire a consultant to provide a critical review. This approach guarantees an independent evaluation. The consultant will find most of the inconsistencies and the marked-up version that is returned to you should pinpoint any problems.

Set Realistic Deadlines

Set deadlines for each stage of your project. When you request a review, you want a response within a specific length of time. Your review request should be written and might include a phrase such as: "If this review is not returned within three days, your corrections will not be included. Review immediately, please."

Everyone involved in your project should be realistic about deadlines, including reviewers. If you know that a reviewer will be unavailable to sign-off the document, find someone else to sign it off.

Keep Track of the Money and Schedule Your Work Flow

What will your user's manual cost and how much time will it take to produce? A work schedule and cost estimate are essential to successful planning. Know your budget. Be sure that money has been budgeted for helpers before you engage them.

Professionals rely on schedules. If you expect to finish the user's manual on time, prepare a realistic production schedule. Whether you use a Gantt chart, PERT, or critical path analysis, make a schedule that shows the work flow from start to finish. Figure 1–2 outlines the major steps in publication planning and production.

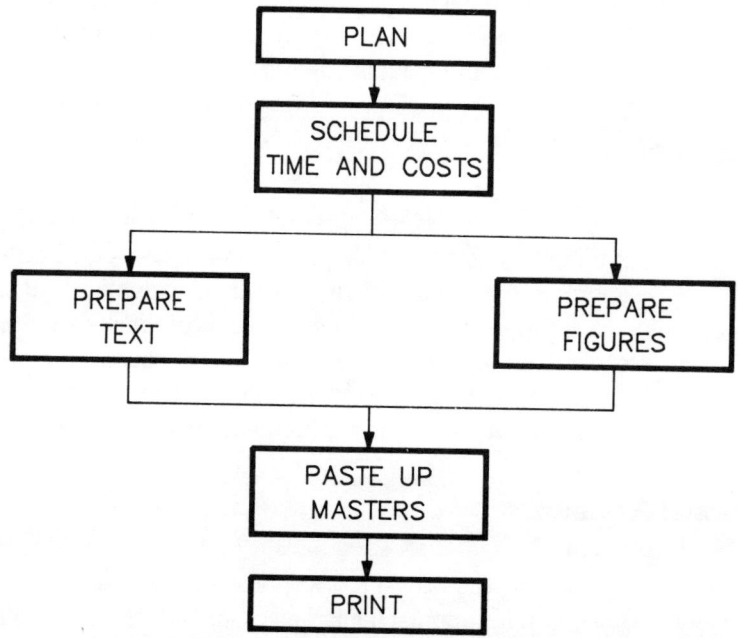

Figure 1–2. Major steps in publications planning and production.

Allow a minimum of three man-months for writing and revising a 100-page user's manual, one month of which is dedicated to review cycles. Allow an additional man-month for preparing a graphics package and for printing the final product. These estimates assume that all goes smoothly. If there are delays, the total time will be longer. Figure 1–3 is an example of a production schedule for a typical user's manual.

Compare the production schedule with the flowchart: the flowchart is time-independent, but the production schedule shows the time required for each task. Many programs produce a project summary. The summary covers man-loading, costs, working times, holidays, start date, and completion date. Refer to Figure 1–4.

```
Typical User's Manual, Revision 83, 8/9/89
Prepared by R.A. McGrath


                               Aug       Sep             Oct    Oct       Nov
                               14  21 28 4   11 18 25 2   9  16 23 30 6    13
Job Description                0   1  2  3   4  5  6  7   8  9  10 11 12   13

   1 Start Work                0   .  .  .   .  .  .  .   .  .  .  .  .    .
   2 Product Briefing/Outline  >=====X   .   .  .  .  .   .  .  .  .  .    .
   3 Draft Copy 1st 1/2        0=========>   .  .  .  .   .  .  .  .  .    .
   4 Customer's Review         .   .  >=====>   .  .  .   .  .  .  .  .    .
   5 Draft Copy 2nd 1/2        .   .  >=========>  .  .   .  .  .  .  .    .
   6 Customer's Review         .   .  .  .   >=====>  .   .  .  .  .  .    .
   7 Prepare Figures/Photos/Illust  .  .  >==============X  .  .  .  .    .
   8 Prepare Revised Draft (All)  .  .  .   .  >==========>  .  .  .  .    .
   9 Customer's Review         .   .  .  .   .  .  >=====X  .  .  .  .    .
  10 Prepare Camera-ready Masters .  .  .   .  .  .  >=======  >  .  .    .
  11 Deliver Camera-ready Masters .  .  .   .  .  .  .   .  *  .  .  .    .
  12 Print Manual              .   .  .  .   .  .  .  .   .  >=========>   .
  13 Tabs/Collate/Binders      .   .  .  .   .  .  .  .   .  >==============X
  14 Adjust                    .   .  .  .   .  .  .  .   .  .  .  >==========>
  15 Deliver Finished Manual   .   .  .  .   .  .  .  .   .  .  .  .  .    X
                Sr Tech. Writer=1  1  1  0   1  1  0  0   0  0  0  0  0    0
               Sr. Tech. Illus.=0  0  1  1   1  0  0  0   0  0  0  0  0    0
              Page Comp. Spec.=0   0  0  0   0  0  1  1   0  0  0  0  0    0
          Total manpower level=1   1  2  1   2  1  1  1   0  0  0  0  0    0
              Manpower cost=1.3K 1.3K 1.3K 2.7K 1.3K 2.7K 1.3K 1.3K 1.3K 0  0  0  0  0
                 Direct cost=0     0  0  0   0  0  0  0   0  0  0  0  0    0
               Total cost=1.3K 1.3K 1.3K 2.7K 1.3K 2.7K 1.3K 1.3K 1.3K 0  0  0  0  0


Symbol - Explanation
>---->     Duration of a normal job
>....>     Slack time for a normal job
>====>     Duration of a critical path job
>::::>     Duration of a completed job
*          Job with zero duration
0---->     Job with no prerequisites
>----X     Job with no successors
```

Figure 1–3. Production schedule for a typical user's manual.

```
                    PROJECT DESCRIPTION REPORT
                    --------------------------
                       Typical User's Manual
                        Revision 83, 8/9/89
                       Prepared by R.A. McGrath
```

```
DESCRIPTION DATA FIELDS:
        Name of project=Typical User's Manual
       Leader of project=O. M.
              Time scale=Weeks
              Start date=8/14/89
      Direct cost units=$
   Manpower cost units=$
    Find critical path=Yes
   File drive and name=a:typmans
```

```
SKILL CATEGORIES:
                          Description        $/Man-Week   Man-Weeks   Total Cost
        1st skill category= Oper. Manager       1440          0          $0
        2nd skill category= Sr Tech. Writer     1380          6         $8.2K
        3rd skill category= Sr. Tech. Illus.    1380          3         $4.1K
        4th skill category= Page Comp. Spec.    1333          2         $2.6K
        5th skill category= Pasteup Artist       600          0          $0
        6th skill category= 1/2 Time Pasteup     300          0          $0
        7th skill category= 1/2 Time Assistant   200          0          $0
        8th skill category=                        0          0          $0
        9th skill category=                        0          0          $0
```

```
WORKING HOURS:
             Begin work=8
            Start lunch=12
           Finish lunch=13
               End work=17
```

```
WORKING DAYS:
     Days of the week=MTuWThF
```

```
HOLIDAYS:
        Holiday list=7/4/89 9/4/89 10/9/89 11/23/89 12/25/89 1/1/90
```

```
SCHEDULE SUMMARY:
       Completion date=11/13/89
        Number of jobs=15
        Total manpower=11 Man-Weeks
         Manpower cost=$15086
           Direct cost=$0
            Total cost=$15086
```

Figure 1–4. Project summary for a typical user's manual.

Several skill categories have been included to allow cost comparison of different types of work. The in-house writer and illustrator have been assigned an arbitrary pay rate of $1,380 per week. The total cost does not reflect printing or packaging expenses, such as binding or the design of covers for the manual.

Set a Freeze Date

After the time and cost schedules have been completed, choose a freeze date. The freeze date is the day after which no additional changes will be incorporated into the manual. There might be more changes needed, but they will have to wait for the next revision.

HAVE YOUR PLAN SIGNED OFF

Have your plan reviewed and signed off by the people who are responsible for production within your company. Everyone must agree to the freeze date. If there are suggestions or corrections, it is easier to make them now rather than later.

SUMMARY OF CHAPTER 1

- Collect or order the tools you will need to do the job.
- Complete the necessary research.
- Prepare an outline.
- Have the outline reviewed, then incorporate the reviewer's suggestions.
- Line up the helpers and services you will need.
- Plan to test your user's manual.
- Make a production schedule and cost estimate.
- Set a freeze date.
- Have your plan signed off.

2

Writing the Main Sections

Chapter 2 begins with a few suggestions about writing for your audience then describes preparation of the three main sections of a user's manual: the Introduction, Ground Rules and Procedures, and Step-by-Step Instructions.

The time required to complete these sections varies, depending upon the complexity of your software. As a rule of thumb, it takes three to four man-months to write a 100-page user's manual, including the review cycles.

SUGGESTIONS ABOUT WRITING

Assume that the reader knows nothing about software or computers rather than write for an advanced professional. As a general rule, write simply and unambiguously.

Define Your Audience

Write for your audience. Pretend that you are explaining your program to a friend and that everything you take for granted is new to the reader. Explain the background necessary to use the software; an accountant, for example, would see a spreadsheet program differently than a graphic designer would.

Little Words Are User-Friendly

Be concise. Use little words that are commonplace. Your words should be crystal clear and ideas should follow a logical order. Avoid using jargon and computerese You might understand jargon, but your reader might not. Make your sentences short. Each sentence should contain one main idea. Stick to your main point and write like a professional—in terms that are easy to understand.

Use Your Outline

After your outline and production schedule are approved and signed off, you're ready to start writing. The outline is your roadmap and the production schedule sets target dates for each stage of the process.

Write your user's manual by expanding the outline. In the material that follows, refer to the outline example in Chapter 1. For now, ignore the Front Matter.

WRITING THE INTRODUCTION

The Introduction should contain an overview of the hardware and software requirements of your program. Provide enough technical information so that the reader can determine whether or not an existing system is adequate.

About the Program

First, address the questions of who, what, where, when, why, and how as they apply to your program. Answering these six questions is a journalist's approach to providing critical information in a small space.

1. Who uses this kind of software?
2. What are the program's special features?
3. Where does the application fit into the user's spectrum of needs?
4. When are the applications most appropriate?
5. Why is this software necessary?
6. How does the program save money, time, or effort?

Then, in two or three sentences, answer each question. Condense the material into a few paragraphs. You do not have to address each question in sequence, however, it may be convenient to do so. The following example shows one way of doing this for a hypothetical software package called "ABC."

ABOUT ABC

ABC software is a combined word processing and graphics program, designed for people who need both words and pictures in their work. This software was developed for writers and publications businesses.

ABC is designed to run on IBM PC/XT personal computers and is distributed on floppy disks. The program saves time because it is easy to use. Everything you will need for writing and illustrating reports and manuals is in one piece of software.

If you already use another word processing program (e.g.,WordStar, WORD, or any program that saves data as ASCII files), you can directly transfer files created with that program into ABC.

ABC works with most mice, joy sticks, and digitizing pads, with over 30 printers (including ink-jet and laser-based printers), and with more than a dozen of the most popular pen plotters.

System Requirements

System requirements and specifications should be discussed individually. Use short, descriptive statements to explain the hardware and software needed to use your program. If some topics are too complex for brief treatment, refer the reader to an Appendix for more information.

Operating System

Describe the operating system(s) that support your software. Is your package preconfigured for a particular computer, or must the reader configure the program before it can be used?

Memory

How much computer memory is necessary to use your program? If different versions of the program require different memory capacities, say so. Distinguish between required and recommended memory sizes.

Disk Drives

How many and what kind of disk drives are needed? Does your program require a hard disk system? How much disk capacity is necessary?

Program Installation

Describe the installation or configuration procedures. Stress the ease of installation. Indicate that step-by-step instructions will be provided in later sections of the manual.

Compatible Computers

List the computers that can run your program. Include brand names and model numbers. For example, instead of "IBM compatible," use "the AT&T 6300 (all models), Compaq Portable," and so on.

Compatible Terminals and Graphics Adapters

List the terminals or graphics adapter cards that work with your program and include the resolution that can be achieved with each. This list should be the same one that appears on the program's configuration menu for terminals or adapter cards.

Compatible Printers and Plotters

List the printers and plotters that work with your program. This list should be the same one that appears on the program's printer or plotter configuration menu. Include model numbers.

Options

Discuss options such as graphics tablets, joy sticks, or light pens, referring the reader to an Appendix for configuration instructions. Use the "Options" heading to describe secondary programs that work with your software, for example, spread-sheet programs that might interface with a graphics package.

Other Specifications

Discuss the distinguishing features of your program. For example, if your software has subroutines for converting data files from other programs, list the types of files that can be converted (e.g., .TXT, .DWG, or .DIF). Briefly describe other programs, if any, that are required to use your software.

The Revision Appendix

If you make software revisions that change the system requirements, describe the changes in a Revision Appendix. Refer the reader to this Appendix.

GROUND RULES AND PROCEDURES

Discuss and illustrate the conventions you plan to follow in your user's manual. Include any cautions or special instructions.

Disks and Disk Handling

Describe the care, handling, and storage of disks. Specify which type of disks are needed to provide sufficient space for your program. Distinguish between double-sided, double-density, and other types of disk.

Standard Caution Symbols

Refer the reader to the back of the disk envelope. Most manufacturers print symbols and cautions on the envelope. It is not necessary to repeat this information.

Power ON . . . Power OFF

In one paragraph explain the importance of following the proper disk insertion and removal sequences. Briefly discuss voltage spikes and surge suppressors. If your program requires that a special disk remains in drive A at all times, say so.

Definitions

Define the conventional disk names. Your company might use nonstandard terminology, but be sure to write definitions that are unambiguous. Disk names are often confusing to novices. If you do not have established terms, use these names:

- System disk: Distinguish between the reader's system disk and the other types of disks that are required.

- Master disk (or Distribution Disk): The value of an unspoiled master disk is well known to experienced computer users, but your reader might be a beginner. Explain why backup disks are necessary. Include this statement: "Use the master disk only to make backup disks."
- Master backup disk: Explain that the master backup disk is like an insurance policy in the event that the master disk is ever damaged. If your program is supplied on multiple disks, explain the need for a complete set of master backup disks.
- Working disk: Explain the necessity for having another backup of the master disk which will be the user's working disk. If your program is supplied on multiple disks, emphasize the need for a complete set of working disks.

Size, Capacity, and Density

If your program is available on different disk sizes, such as 8", 5 ¼", or 3 ½", tell the reader what is available. If a hard disk can (or must) be used, describe any features that might seem unusual to a new user. Prepare a line drawing to show the parts of your disk package. Refer to Figure 2–1.

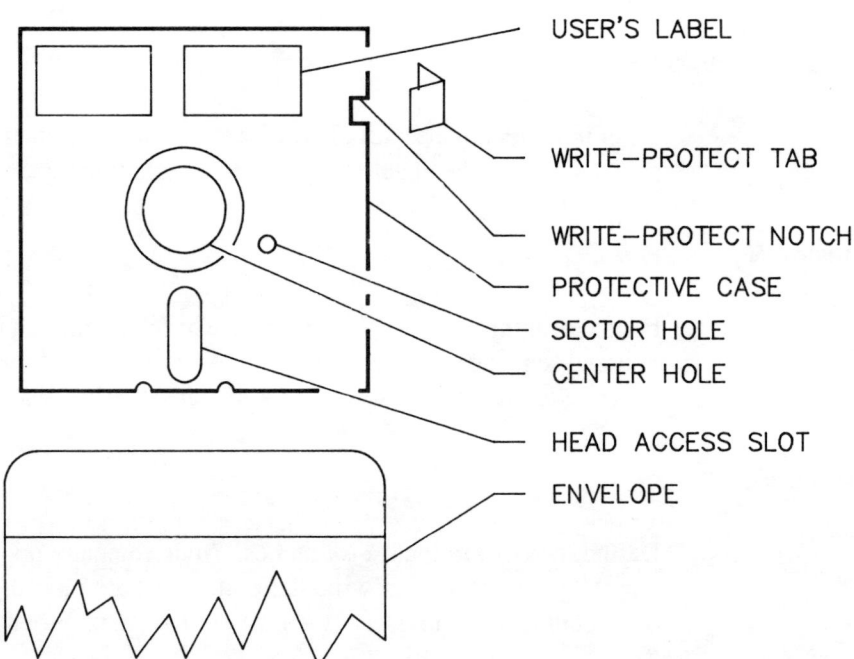

Figure 2–1. Parts of a 5 ¼" disk package.

Conventions

Define any special names or symbols used with your program. Illustrate each of the terms. For example, define "booting a system" and "A:>"

Instruction Example

Provide a preview of the language you plan to use for instructions. Refer to the following example:

BOOTING YOUR SYSTEM

Insert your system disk into drive A. Latch the disk drive door.

Switch your computer and terminal ON. (Wait a few moments.)

On the screen you'll see ENTER NEW DATE:

Press: **RETURN**

On the screen you'll see ENTER NEW TIME:

Press: **RETURN**

On the screen you'll see
A:>

Key Commands

List and define any special commands. Distinguish between commands such as "Type:" and "Press:." Explain the difference between an ESCAPE and a CONTROL command. Give an example of each type of command and use boldface type or a box around the name of the command key. Refer to Figure 2–2.

PRESS ONE KEY   PRESS TOGETHER

F3   SHIFT   ESC — S

Figure 2-2. Illustrating keystrokes.

Filenames

Make a list of filenames as they appear in the directory of your distribution disk. After each filename give a brief description. If you make revisions or add new files, describe the changes in the Revision Appendix. Refer to the following example:

ABC FILENAMES

. . .
< GRA.SWP> The graphics swap file moves data between a disk and your computer's random access memory (RAM).
< GRA.TXT> The graphics text file merges graphics data into a text file.
< SAMP.DWG> A drawing example.
< TEST 3> A file for checking printer configuration and operation.

. . .

Filenames should appear in the same order shown on the display when a directory command is executed. Discuss the naming of files and file extensions. Use angle brackets < > or a different type style to distinguish filenames and extensions from other text. The brackets mean: "a file named . . .," for example, ". . .when you refer to < SAMP.DWG> be sure to . . .".

Keyboard—Screen Instruction Example

Provide a preview of the language you will use for keyboard and screen instructions. Refer to the following example:

THE KEYBOARD AND THE SCREEN

Keyboard instructions and the messages on the screen will be in this form:

Type: GRA.TXT

Press: **RETURN**

On the screen you'll see GRAPHICS FILENAME?

Type: B:AVG.GRA

Screen Representation

Referring to the screen as the "CRT," "tube," "display," and "monitor" can be confusing to the reader. A variety of words might be preferable in literary writing, but in a user's manual, variety is confusing. The word "screen" should be adequate for most applications.

Discuss the cursor and its movement. Describe, as appropriate, scrolling, panning, fields, TAB to field, and use of the function and arrow keys. If a mouse, digitizing tablet, or light pen is used, describe its operation.

If the screen displays only a few prompt lines, insert the information in the text. If the screen response is more complex, illustrate the screen. You can show only the upper or lower half of the screen in order to save space. Refer to Figure 2–3.

STEP-BY-STEP INSTRUCTIONS

Step-by-step instructions are used to lead your reader through procedures that might be complex and confusing if described in paragraphs of text. Notice the main features common to all step-by-step instructions:

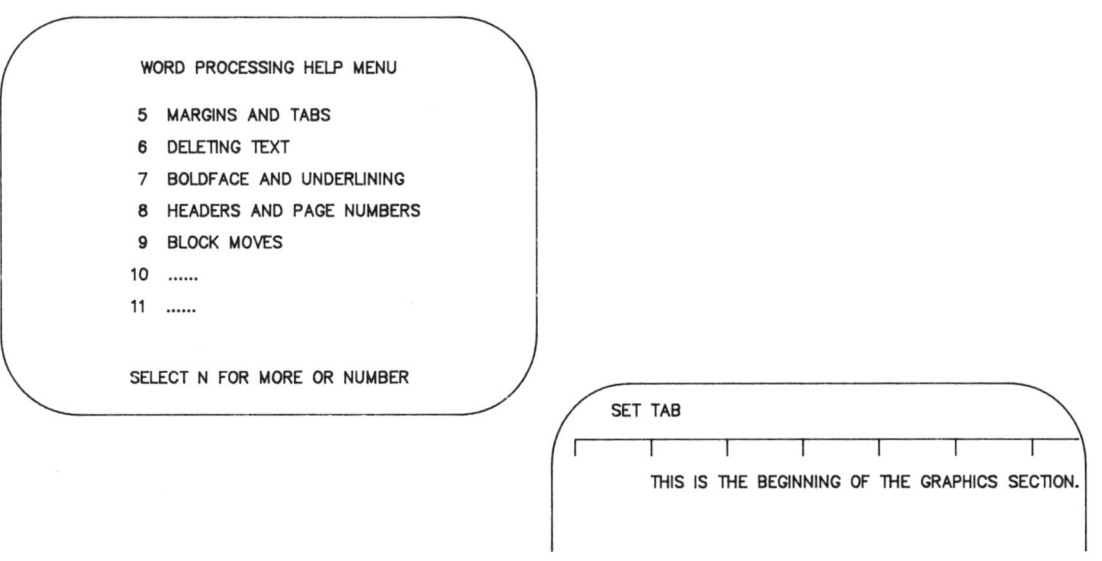

Figure 2–3. (*Left*) Line drawing of full screen. (*Right*) Line drawing of upper part of screen.

- Each step is short. The first word is usually an action verb, telling the reader to do something.
- NOTEs and CAUTIONs are located *before* the step to which they apply. Use a consistent format to show these items. NOTEs are informational. CAUTIONs deal with safety. Refer to the following examples:

> **NOTE:** Apply a write-protect tab to your disk after making the backup copy.

> **CAUTION:**   Unplug the computer and monitor before you begin this procedure.

- Each task is assigned to a single step. Avoid using several steps in one instruction.
- The language is consistent. There is no confusion.

Make a Backup Disk

Begin with an easy first task so that the reader can become accustomed to your writing style. Because making a backup disk is a required procedure, it is a good starting exercise. The following is an example:

TO BACKUP YOUR MASTER DISK

> **NOTE:** Refer to the instructions in your computer operator's guide for disk formatting instructions.

Boot your system.

Insert your master (distribution) disk into drive A and latch the disk drive door. Insert a formatted disk into drive B.

Type: COPY *.* B: Press **RETURN**.

(Wait until the copying is finished). Remove your backup disk from drive B. Label the backup disk "Master backup disk." Put the master backup disk into its envelope and store the disk in a safe place.

Remove your master disk from drive A. Put the master disk into its envelope and store the disk in a safe place.

In preliminary examples, list every step of the procedure. When the reader is familiar with your writing style, you can shorten the procedures. For example, later in the manual you might use "Make a backup of your disk" to cover this procedure.

Start-up Instructions

Start-up instructions represent the reader's first encounter with your program. Refer to the following example:

STARTING THE ABC PROGRAM

Boot your system.

Insert your working disk into drive A and latch the disk drive door.

Type: GO. Press: **RETURN**. On the screen you'll see

In a few moments the copyright screen will be replaced by the START-UP MENU. On the screen you'll see

```
                    START-UP  MENU

                 1   HELP
                 2   CONFIGURE  ABC
                 3   WORD  PROCESSING
                 4   DRAW  GRAPHICS
                 5   PLOT  GRAPHICS
                 6   USE  PRINTER
                 7   CONVERT  ASCII  FILE


             SELECT  N  FOR  MORE  OR  NUMBER
```

Some of the steps in your program will be different from the ones in the examples. However, the purpose of the examples is only to provide a model for describing these procedures, so make whatever modifications are appropriate for your program.

Installing a Graphics Adapter Card

If your program does not require configuration, explain this in one sentence. If your program requires configuring for a terminal or graphics adapter card, use an approach such as the following:

SELECTING THE GRAPHICS ADAPTER CARD

> **NOTE:** This procedure assumes that your system has been booted and that the START-UP MENU appears on the screen.

Type: 2 Press: **RETURN**

The START-UP MENU will be replaced with the ADAPTER CARD CONFIGURATION MENU. On the screen you'll see

```
        ADAPTER CARD CONFIGURATION MENU

            1   IBM (320 X 200)

            2   IBM ENHANCED GRAPHICS

            3   HERCULES COLOR

            4   .....

            5   .....

            6   .....

            7   TECMAR (640 X 400) COLOR


        SELECT N FOR MORE OR NUMBER
```

Select the number corresponding to the card you are using.   For example, to select "7,"

Type: 7. Press: **RETURN**. On the screen you'll see

TEST THE TECMAR CONFIGURATION? (Y/N)

Type: Y

A series of test patterns will appear on your screen. If you have selected the incorrect card for your system, on the screen you'll see:

ERROR CODE: TC-3
TO RETURN TO CONFIGURATION MENU, TYPE A

Type: A

Look at the menu and select the correct graphics adapter card number. If your card is not on the menu, refer to Appendix II for special configuration instructions. If you have selected the correct adapter card, on the screen you'll see

TEST FOR TECMAR GRAPHICS MASTER OK.
TO SAVE THIS CONFIGURATION, PRESS **RETURN.**

Press: **RETURN**

On the screen you'll see the START-UP MENU

Installing Input Devices

Procedures for selecting mice, digitizing tablets, and light pens are similar to those for selecting adapter cards. Include this section if it is necessary. An Appendix should illustrate cabling diagrams for the connectors used with each input device. If more than one input device is required, describe the configuration for each one.

Input devices have differing levels of complexity. For example, a joy stick might require a game adapter card. You are obliged to describe installation of the adapter card if your software package supports a joy stick that requires the card. In addition, adapter cards often have switches or jumpers that must be set for proper operation. Is it your job to describe the switch settings? As another example, consider the serial mouse. Although the installation is quite simple, the serial port must be configured to the correct baud rate and communications protocol or the mouse will not work at all. In addition, there is often a special utility program that is used to set up the mouse buttons. How much information should you provide?

Installation and configuration issues are often nested in layers of never-ending complexity. One way to deal with this problem is to mention the issues (e.g., the switches, jumpers, or utility programs) and then refer your reader to the user's manual provided by the equipment manufacturer. If the manufacturer's documentation is incorrect or incomplete, you should provide your user with some tips and hints that will make it easier to install or configure the device.

Installing a Printer or Plotter

The instructions for configuring printers and plotters are very similar. In either case, refer the reader to the proper Appendix for more details. The Appendix should include cabling diagrams for the connector to each kind of printer or plotter that is supported. If more than one output device is required, describe the configuration for each device. Refer to the following example:

SELECTING THE PRINTER

Boot your system and start ABC.

Type: 2.   Press: **RETURN**

The START-UP MENU will be replaced with the PRINTER CONFIGURATION MENU. On the screen you'll see

```
        PRINTER CONFIGURATION MENU

     1   ANADEX 6500

     2   ANADEX 9000, 9500

     3   C. ITOH  (ALL SERIES)

     4   EPSON MX-100

     5   EPSON FX- (ALL SERIES)

     6   IBM COLOR PRINTER

     7   IDS PRISM 80


        SELECT N FOR MORE OR NUMBER
```

Select the number corresponding to the printer you're using. For example, if yours is an Epson MX-100, select "4" on the menu.

Type: 4. Press: **RETURN**

On the screen you'll see

DO YOU WANT TO TEST THE EPSON MX-100 CONFIGURATION? (Y/N)

Type: Y

On the screen you'll see

SWITCH YOUR PRINTER ON, INSERT PAPER, THEN PRESS RETURN.

> **NOTE:** Different printers have different requirements, e.g., a warming up period.

Switch your printer ON.

Insert paper into your printer. Press: **RETURN**
An automatic program will test your printer. When the test is finished, on the screen you'll see

```
                    PRINTER  TEST  DISPLAY

     123456789012345          123456789012345
      123456789012345          123456789012345
       123456789012345          123456789012345
        123456789012345          123456789012345
         123456789012345          123456789012345
          123456789012345          123456789012345
           123456789012345          123456789012345
            123456789012345          123456789012345
```

If you selected the correct printer for your program, the printout will correspond exactly to what is shown on the screen. To SAVE your printer configuration, Type: Y

If you selected an incorrect printer number, the printout will not correspond to the pattern shown on the display.
Type: N

Look at the menu again and select the correct printer identification number. If your printer is not on the menu, refer to Appendix III for printer configuration instructions.

The HELP MENU

The HELP MENU should be easy to use. When a reader seeks help, the required information should be found directly, without the need for several screens of information being scrolled through.

Start with a Simple Example

The reader now has software configured for the graphics adapter card, an input device, and a printer or plotter. It is time to provide the tools for finding more information within the program. Describe use of the HELP MENU. Refer to the following example:

USING THE HELP MENU

The HELP MENU can be called up at any time. To access the HELP MENU, press: F1

If, for example, you are writing a letter and you want to know how to move a paragraph from one place to another, but you have forgotten the commands, do this:

Press: **F1**

The letter that you are writing will temporarily disappear. On the screen you'll see

```
            WORD  PROCESSING  HELP  MENU


        5   MARGINS  AND  TABS
        6   DELETING  TEXT

        7   BOLDFACE  AND  UNDERLINING

        8   HEADERS  AND  PAGE  NUMBERS

        9   BLOCK  MOVES

       10   ......

       11   ......


        SELECT  N  FOR  MORE  OR  NUMBER
```

Select the number corresponding to the topic in question: because you want to know about block moves, select number 9 on the SUBMENU.

Type: 9

On the screen you will see a description of all block move commands. Locate the information you need and then Press: **ESCAPE**

The letter that you were writing will reappear on the screen and you can then move the paragraph.

Other HELP Options

Define each HELP option. Use the same wording as in your Glossary definitions.
Sometimes it is useful to reproduce the entire HELP file as an Appendix.

Tutorial Examples

It is important that the reader have a feeling of success as quickly as possible. One
way to do this is to select tutorial examples that will provide printouts. First, discuss
the SAVE operation, then descibe the printout procedure. Refer to the following
example.

SAVING YOUR WORK

> **NOTE**: Unless you SAVE, when the com-
> puter is RESET or switched OFF, your work
> will be lost.

Press: **F5**

On the screen you'll see

SAVING . . .

The "SAVING . . ." prompt will blink on and off several
times, depending upon the length of your file. When your
program is SAVEd, on the screen you'll see:

FILE SAVED

You can now continue working, print out your results, or
switch your computer OFF without losing your work.

Printout Instructions

The reader has thus far installed the graphics adapter card and printer, used the HELP
MENU, and learned how to SAVE. The printout provides concrete evidence that
something has been accomplished.

PRINTING YOUR WORK

SAVE your work. You can not PRINT unless your data has been SAVEd.

Press: **F6**. On the screen you'll see

```
                    PRINT MENU

          C   CONFIGURE NEW PRINTER
          M   MODIFY PRINT PARAMETERS
          P   PRINT
          S   START AT PAGE ...
          H   PRINT HOW MANY COPIES...
          L   LIST PRINTER CHARACTERISTICS
          F   SINGLE SHEETS


          SELECT N FOR MORE OR LETTER
```

For now, ignore the various options on the PRINT MENU.

Type: P

On the screen you'll see

NAME OF FILE TO PRINT

> **NOTE:** The file that you wish to print is called: < SAMP.DAT>. Type the filename only. Do not type the dot or the file extension.

Type: SAMP

Press: **RETURN**

On the screen you'll see:

READY TO PRINT: SAMP.DAT

INSERT PAPER AND SWITCH YOUR PRINTER ON,
THEN PRESS **RETURN**

Be sure that the paper is properly installed.

Switch your printer ON.

Press: **RETURN**

< SAMP.DAT> will be printed.

After the reader has a printout in hand, explain the purpose and action of each option such as "Start at page" or "Print how many copies?" Do not make the reader guess what to do next. Explain the entire menu.

Other Tutorial Examples

There is no point in printing a complete user's manual in this book. Use the preceding examples as models to explain each of the remaining tutorial sections of your manual. To make your examples easy to understand, follow these guidelines:

- Start at the beginning (with the computer switched OFF), or define the conditions on the screen (e.g., START-UP MENU, A:>, etc.).
- Describe what to do with the equipment, such as, "Switch the computer ON," or "Insert paper into printer."
- Describe what to do at the keyboard (e.g., press: **RETURN, ESCAPE, F3,** or **CTRL–B**.
- Show what appears on the screen. If the screen response is no longer than a few lines, insert them into the text. If the screen display is complex, show a full-or half-screen.
- Describe what to do next. This step is normally a "Move," "Press:," or "Type:" instruction.
- Describe the result.
- Continue to the end of the example.

One feature that makes a user's manual easy to use is consistency. The objective is to provide instructions that are specific and unambiguous. Refer to your outline so that your goals remain in focus.

The tutorial examples are, perhaps, the most important set of instructions in your user's manual because these are the procedures by which your reader comes to understand your program.

Exit the Program

Show the reader how to exit your program. Include all steps needed to shut down the system. The following is a partial example:

SHUTTING DOWN YOUR SYSTEM

...

Switch your computer OFF.

Switch your printer OFF.

Check your work area to be sure that all of your disks are stored in a safe place.

...

Correct and Review Your User's Manual

If you have followed your outline from Chapter 1 and the instructions in Chapter 2, you should have the rough draft of your user's manual almost finished, with the exception of the Front Matter and Back Matter.

Print out your rough draft. Make the corrections that are obvious to you. Now it is time for feedback. Make two or three copies of your rough draft and pass them along to your reviewers, who will provide new input. Decide which comments to include and which to omit. Save all of the reviewers' comments. In Chapter 3 you will learn how to complete the Front Matter and Back Matter. You can work on these sections while the reviewers are busy.

SUMMARY OF CHAPTER 2

- Write simply and unambiguously.
- Start with the Introduction.
- Define the Ground Rules and Conventions.
- Prepare the Step-by-Step Instructions.
- Print out a rough draft of the main sections.
- Send the main sections to the reviewers.

3

Writing the Back Matter and Front Matter

Chapter 3 covers the beginning and ending sections of a user's manual. Once the main body of the manual has been written, complete the Back Matter (except for the Index), and then prepare the Front Matter (with a preliminary Table of Contents). It is advantageous to work on the Back Matter and Front Matter while the main sections are being reviewed.

BACK MATTER

Back Matter consists of reference material that is located at the end of the user's manual. Prepare this section before the Front Matter because it is more complex and contains vital information about the software. Refer to the outline in Chapter 1.

The Reference Guide

The Reference Guide provides a listing of all the commands used in your program. If your program uses only a few commands, include this section in the Back Matter. If there are hundreds of commands, make the Reference Guide a separate manual.

Command Listing

At the beginning of the Reference Guide, provide a complete listing of all commands, indicating the page numbers where the commands can be found. This listing functions as a Table of Contents for the Reference Guide. It is sometimes convenient to make additional lists of menu-related commands with tree diagrams, that show the relationships among the various commands.

Conventions for Describing Commands

Describe commands in alphabetical sequence. If certain commands can be grouped by menus or submenus, note this at the beginning of the description. Include variations of each command (e.g., optional extensions), and refer the reader to related commands. If the command is complex, provide an example. Use a half-page or full-page for each command. Refer to the following example:

MOVE (Graphics Selection Menu)

Submenu	None
Variations:	None
Required Commands:	**POINT** or **FRAME**
Related Commands:	**COPY, ROTATE, MIRROR**

MOVE is used to relocate an entity or image to another position on the screen. Before **MOVE** can be executed, the entity or image must be identified. This is accomplished by pointing (see **POINT**) or framing (see **FRAME**).

After identifying the entity or image, select **MOVE** from the screen menu. Reposition the cursor at the screen location to which the object will be moved. The object will follow the cursor. Press the left mouse button (or **RETURN**) to attach the object at the new location. The entity or image will disappear from the previous location.

Error Codes

Throughout your instructions and examples, you have undoubtedly referred to Error Codes. Rather than describe or explain each Error Code in the instructions, put them into a table or list. The Error Codes are easy to find in this format. In defining Error Codes, three items are needed per entry:

- Error Code Identification
- Description
- Recovery Action

Error Code Listing

Short, concise explanations are best. The objective is to provide the reader with a solution to a problem quickly. Make your statements brief and to the point. Refer to the following example:

ERROR CODE LIST

ERROR CODE	DESCRIPTION	RECOVERY ACTION
. . .	. . .	. . .
E–3	Swap file full	D
E–4	Disk full	B, G, H, I
E–5	File already exists	B, C
E–6	Incorrect filename	B, C
. . .	. . .	. . .

Recovery Action List

For a complex program, too much space is required to write each Recovery Action in the table, especially when several actions are repeated. One solution is to prepare a separate Recovery Action List and to append the description of Recovery Actions to the Error Code listing. Refer to the following example:

RECOVERY ACTION LIST

ACTION	DESCRIPTION
A	Check to be sure that power is ON.
B	Refer to file directory.
C	Select new filename or file extension.
D	SAVE immediately and reopen file.
E	Rename file or file extension.
F	Remove disk and try backup disk.
G	Erase unnecessary files.
H	Move files to another disk.
I	. . .

If additional Recovery Actions are needed, use "AA," "BB," or "CC," and so on, to indicate these actions. Your Error Code List and Recovery Actions might span several pages. Make the table understandable, regardless of its length.

Appendices

Each Appendix must be identified. You can use "APPENDIX 1" or "APPENDIX I," or "APPENDIX A." Assign a separate Appendix for each topic. Identify Appendices "1, 2, 3, 4 . . . ," "I, II, III, IV . . . ," or "A, B, C, D . . . ," but make the identifying characters consistent.

An Appendix is the place for special instructions. For example, the procedure for configuring the program for a special printer or terminal belongs there. Appendix instructions should be written in the same style as instructions that appear within your text because the reader might be confused by a change in style. Appendix entries that consist of lists or tables are brief and concise.   Refer to the following example:

APPENDICES

APPENDIX	DESCRIPTION
Appendix I	Revision Summary by Date
Appendix II	Configuring Unlisted Terminals
Appendix III	Configuring Unlisted Printers
Appendix IV	Configuring Pen Plotters
Appendix V	Configuring Input Devices
Appendix VI	Modification of Default Values
Appendix VII	. . .

Glossary

The Glossary is a dictionary. Use the Glossary to explain any special terms, as well as the common computer words that appear in your manual. Refer to the following procedure for building a Glossary and see the example:

- Read through your user's manual and highlight each word or term that might be unfamiliar to your reader.
- Create a separate word processing file for the Glossary.
- Enter each highlighted word or term on a separate line in the Glossary file.
- Capitalize each term.
- Skip a line between each entry.
- Alphabetize your list and eliminate duplicate entries.

- Either refer to a computer dictionary or create a brief definition for each entry in your list.
- Include definitions for abbreviated terms next to their abbreviations, or refer the reader to the complete nomenclature. For example: RAM. See Random Access Memory.

GLOSSARY EXAMPLE

. . .

Joy Stick. A control device that moves left, right, forward, and back. It is used to move a cursor around on the screen rapidly.

Keyboard. An array of buttons that, when pressed, converts mechanical movement into electrical signals for computer processing.

Laser Printer. A class of high-speed printing machines that generate hardcopy by using laser-based technology.

. . .

Index

The Index is a listing of important words, ideas, and concepts in your user's manual. Page numbers indicate where each item can be found. An Index is a necessary part of your manual because it enables the reader to find specific topics that can not be located from the Table of Contents. The Index is one of the last items to be completed because it can be compiled only after page numbers have been assigned.

In preparing the Index, use a program such as INDEX (Digital Marketing) or WORD (Microsoft). It is not worth the time or effort to prepare the Index manually. If no other option is available, hire a technical writer to create the Index for you.

Readers' Response Card

Readers' Response Cards benefit you, the software publisher, and the reader. The purpose of the card is to provide an easy-to-use method by which readers can supply feedback about the user's manual.

- The Readers' Response Card helps users because they feel that you care about their ideas and comments.
- The card helps you to understand the weaknesses of your user's manual, which you can correct in a later revision.

- The card helps your publisher or your company because it provides a data base for a mailing list.

Provide two to four Readers' Response Cards, separated by perforations so that the cards can be removed easily. A user's manual may pass through many hands. The more people who have a chance to respond, the more feedback you can get. You will receive more responses if the questions are brief and the card does not require a long time to complete. Include these items:

- Respondent's name and title.
- Space for the date.
- Complete business address.
- Checkbox for: "Is this manual easy to use?" (Yes/No)
- Checkbox for: "How would you rate this manual?" (Good/Fair/Poor)
- Space (one line) for: "What do you like most about this manual?"
- Space (one line) for: "What do you like least about this manual?"
- Space for: "Additional comments."
- On the address side of the card, include your company's name, the full return address, and postage.

FRONT MATTER

Front Matter consists of all material that appears before the Introduction. These items are:

- Title Page and Copyright Notice (can be separate pages)
- Acknowledgments
- License Agreement and Notice of Disclaimer
- Table of Contents and List of Figures
- Supplementary Manuals

Title Page

The first page of a user's manual should contain the following information:

- The exact title of the program.
- A brief subtitle that describes the program.
- The name of the company that is producing or distributing the program.
- Revision number of the program.
- Copyright Notice and date (sometimes placed on the second page)

Usually, your company or a software distribution house has an established format for the Title Page. If this is not the case, use the Title Page of this book as an example.

Acknowledgments

The rule for Acknowledgments is this: if someone provides significant help, say so. It is better to err on the side of more Acknowledgments rather than to hurt someone's feelings (or create possible grounds for legal action) by leaving a name out of the section. Acknowledge the people who helped with the research, writing, or production of the manual. In some cases it is appropriate to include the venture capital firm or individuals who funded a project. Include a listing of brand names and trademarks in this section.

Agreement and Disclaimer

Use a separate page for the License Agreement and Notice of Disclaimer. You will need to reserve a page and figure number for the Agreement Card that the reader can fill out and return to you. The Agreement should be perforated so that it can be removed easily from the manual. Print the Agreement on the same thickness of card stock as the Readers' Response Card. On the address side of the card, include your company's return address and provide postage.

Obtain approval from your lawyer (or your company's legal staff) of the exact wording of the Copyright Notice, License Agreement, and Notice of Disclaimer. Use the language that your attorney advises.

Table of Contents

The Table of Contents is a directory for the chapters and sections of your manual. Unlike the Index, which deals with specific topics, the Table of Contents provides an overview of the material.

If using software to generate the Index and Table of Contents, work directly from the word processing file that contains the manual. Insert into the file the special characters used to distinguish among chapters, sections, headings, and subheadings wherever these items occur. Refer to the software that you are using for the correct special characters.

Save the Table of Contents to a separate file for subsequent editing. As you make the final formatting adjustments to the manual, the Table of Contents will be automatically updated to include, for example, changes in section names or movement of a section from one page to another.

If you do the job manually, you can construct a Table of Contents from your outline, if you have kept the outline updated. If the outline is different from what you have written, read through your manual and copy the names of sections, headings, and subheadings—exactly as they appear in the text. Leave the page numbers blank until formatting of the manual is finished, then add the correct page numbers.

There are several basic styles for a Table of Contents. Two examples follow:

EXAMPLE 1

EXAMPLE 2

List of Figures

The List of Figures is a tool with which a reader can locate an illustration in your manual. Figure numbers reflect the section where the figure is located. For example, Figure 4–2 is the second figure in section 4. Put the section number first, then a hyphen (or en dash), then the sequential figure number within that section.

Every line drawing, photograph, or cartoon should be assigned a figure number and included in the List of Figures. Create a column for the page numbers. Enter the page numbers after the pages are assigned for the Table of Contents. Refer to the following example:

LIST OF FIGURES

Figure	Title	Page
1–1	Flowchart of publications project	1–2
1–2	Production schedule	1–3
1–3	Project summary	1–4
2–1	Disk parts	2–5

Supplementary Manuals

It is possible that your manual will be part of a set or series. For example: a Programmer's Guide might be required for certain applications, or another software package might be necessary to run your program. This kind of information is too important to be hidden inside the manual. List the Supplementary Manuals in the Front Matter and discuss the necessary software in the Introduction under "System Requirements."

When listing related manuals, include identifying numbers, manufacturers, and dates of latest revisions. After the list of Supplementary Manuals, a blank page should appear before the beginning of the main sections of your user's manual.

MAKE SURE EVERYTHING AGREES

The three final steps before starting production are the crosscheck, sign-off, and freeze. These items refer to the main sections as well as to the Front Matter and Back Matter.

Crosscheck

Carefully review the Front Matter and Back Matter. The numbers and references must agree. Review the main body of the manual and eliminate all references to specific page numbers except in the Index, Table of Contents, and List of Figures. If you must refer to something elsewhere in your manual, refer to it by chapter or section—not by page number.

Check each line of the entire document for correct spelling, punctuation, and grammar. References to figures and examples must agree with the numbers assigned to these items. Crosscheck the Appendices against Appendix references in the body of the manual.

Sign-off for Production

Complete the final review of your manual and collect the sign-off sheets from your reviewers. You are ready to start production of the manual.

Freeze the Document

Once your manual has cleared the final review, do not accept any further changes. Insist on this point. Errors must be corrected, of course, but adding a new feature to the software is different from correcting a mistake.

SUMMARY OF CHAPTER 3

- Work on the Back Matter and Front Matter while the other sections are being reviewed.
- Complete the Back Matter first, then the Front Matter.
- Crosscheck all entries.
- Collect the sign-offs from your reviewers.
- Freeze the document.

4

Production

Chapter 4 covers the transition from final drafts of text and sketches to the camera-ready master copies that your printer will use to produce finished user's manuals. Figure 4–1 shows the major production steps.

For a typical manual of approximately one hundred pages, allow at least one man-month to prepare inked line drawings, to format text (or to obtain typeset copy), and to paste up the masters.

THREE DIFFERENT APPROACHES

There are three basic types of user's manuals: the most expensive is the typeset manual; the least expensive is the manual that looks like it was prepared with a typewriter. The third alternative is the laser-typography manual, which is of near-typeset quality, and has a professional look but, costs one tenth of the price of typeset copy. There are several ways to produce each of these types of manuals.

The Printer Does It All

The full-service approach is worth considering if you do not want to prepare camera-ready masters or if your company has an in-house graphics and printing

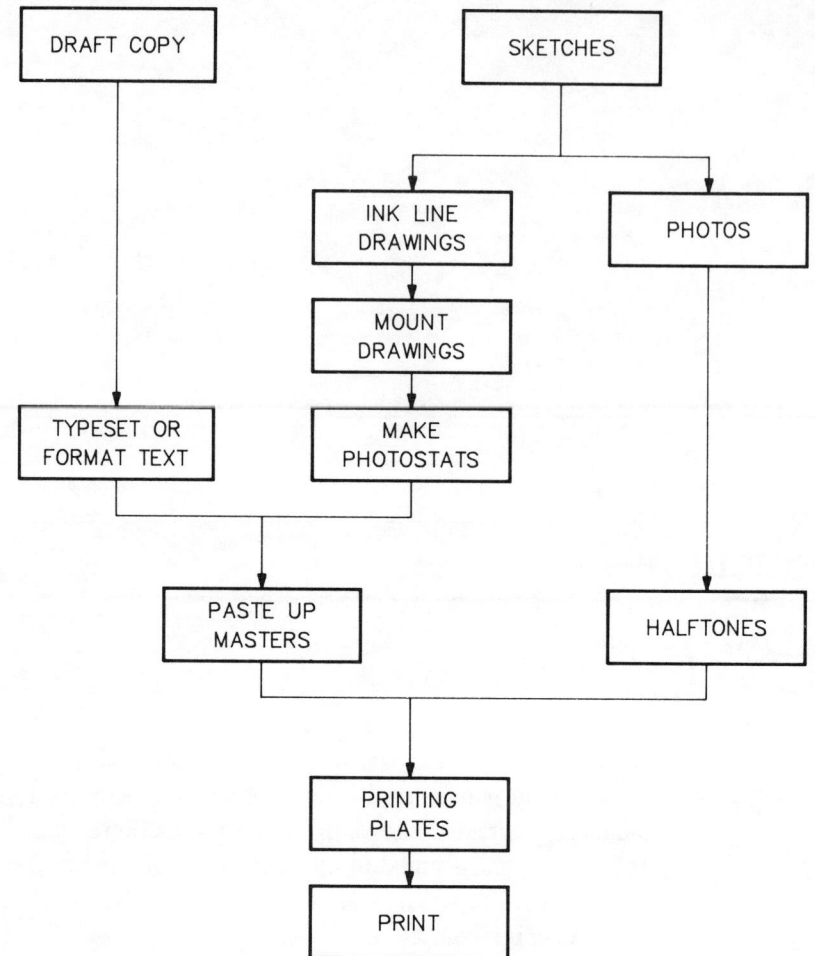

Figure 4-1. Flowchart shows major steps in production of user's manual.

department. With this approach, you need to prepare only a final version of the text and sketches of the figures. The printer supervises typesetting, preparation of inked line drawings, pasteup of the camera-ready masters, and printing of the manual. The advantages of this approach are these:

- Convenience

- Fast, professional service

- No graphics skills or equipment required

- Excellent looking product

It is necessary to check the printer's work at several stages and to make some decisions, such as the size of the finished manual, the materials used for the binding, the paper and type styles, and the number of copies to be produced. After you have paid the bills or cross-charges, the job is finished.

The "Typewriter Manual"

The least expensive approach is to prepare a "typewriter manual." If done carefully, this style of manual is a good choice for software that is being released for the first time because changes can easily be made and revisions are inexpensive. Preparation must be done carefully to ensure a professional product. The procedure is:

- Format the text on your word processor, leaving space for the figures.
- Prepare inked line drawings, or hire an illustrator to prepare them for you.
- Tape each figure onto a mounting board so that it can be handled easily.
- Have a commercial graphics house photostat each figure.
- Paste up the camera-ready masters.
- Send the camera-ready masters to the printer.

The Hybrid Manual

Between the full-service approach and the "typewriter manual" is a hybrid production technique: using either typeset text or laser-based typography, and a combination of your skills and those of contractors, you can prepare the camera-ready masters for the printer, save a lot of money, and still produce a professional looking user's manual.

PRODUCING TEXT

At the present time, typesetting generates the highest quality of text, whereas laser-typography represents the direction of electronic publishing for the future. The following is a comparison of text production methods, which gives special attention to word processed output because this approach is an often-used and inexpensive production technique. Word processing methods can be combined with laser-based printing to create manuals of excellent quality.

Typesetting

Most of today's typesetting is handled in a conventional way: the printer (or typesetter) receives a copy of the text to be typeset, the material is entered into a computer-based typesetting machine, and a strip of typeset text (called a *galley*) is produced as output.

Typeset Galleys

The typeset galley is well suited for multicolumn pages, such as those in magazines. Typeset material can be pasted up in an infinite variety of formats, and figures can be inserted where desired. Typesetting, however, is costly to produce and labor-intensive at the pasteup stage.

If corrections on one page are extensive, the ripple effect can be devastating. For example, if a figure is deleted, the words that follow the figure must be relocated to fill the blank space. Text from the following page—and possibly from several other pages—must be relocated. This movement of text may change the placement of section headings which, in turn, will affect the Table of Contents and the Index.

Full-Page Typeset Text

Full pages of typeset text are more convenient to paste up than single-column galleys. The labor cost of preparing the full-page format is relatively high and most of the dollars go to the typesetter. Multicolumn full-page typesetting is possible, however, but this should only be specified by experienced page designers.

Computer-Generated Typesetting Variations

To reduce typesetting costs, some commercial typesetters offer the following service: If you provide a disk file containing the material to be typeset (or if you transmit the data over a modem) the typesetter will provide galleys made from your direct input at reduced cost. The cost savings occur because material on electronic or magnetic media does not require a keyboard operator to enter the data into the typesetting machine.

In addition, if you are willing to insert the typesetting codes (a special collection of formatting characters, generated at your word processor's keyboard) the costs are even lower. There is a catch, though: if you make a mistake in the coding, the typesetter will not absorb the cost of redoing the work.

Pagination

With conventional typesetting it is difficult to keep track of page numbers until the job is finished. Therefore, the Index, List of Figures, and Table of Contents are usually completed after typesetting and (if you are using a multicolumn format) after the manual is pasted up.

Word Processed Output

The main advantage of a "typewriter manual" is the freedom it provides from typesetting and its complexity. The quality of text on the printed page depends upon your letter-quality printer and the typestyle selected. If you have a good printing device, the image can be excellent.

Word Processed Galleys

If you are using word processed output, the simplest way to produce the text for multicolumn manuals is to print a long galley with margins set to the column width. The pasteup operation of such a galley is identical to that of typeset copy. With this approach, however, final pagination cannot be determined until the pasteup operation is completed.

Full-Page Formatted Text

The ability to produce word processed copy with fully formatted pages is largely a function of the word processing software. Few current programs are satisfactory for multicolumn work. Software like WordStar or Microsoft's WORD (and many others) produce satisfactory single-column, full-page output with letter-quality printers.

Pagination

A distinct advantage of word processing output over conventional typesetting is the ease of generating an Index, Table of Contents, and List of Figures before pasteup of the masters. If blank spaces are provided for the figures, the page numbers are current as the manual is being prepared, and Table of Contents generators or indexing software can be used.

Laser Typography

Laser-based typography represents the future of electronic publishing. As costs decrease and resolution increases, this approach will replace some existing technologies. Word processing programs with drivers for laser-based printers are required to use this technique. However, translation programs are available to transfer older word processing (or ASCII) files to word processing software with the necessary drivers.

This book is an example of laser typography. The original text was produced with an older version of WordStar. Text files were downloaded into Ventura, reformatted, and laser-typeset at a resolution of 400 × 800 dots per inch (dpi).

Background and Future

At present, the resolution of affordable laser engines (300 × 300 dpi) is adequate for text but not for complex graphics. However, in the $20,000—$60,000 price range, laser typesetters that produce resolutions of over 1,200 dpi are available. For most books, reports, and manuals, laser typesetting has become the method of choice for producing camera-ready masters. Conventional typesetting and pen plotting continue to be used, but only for specialty applications.

Full-Page Typography

Several word processing programs are suited for formatting full pages of text for laser typography, such as WordStar 2000, Word Perfect, and WORD. Similar programs are being developed constantly to take advantage of this growing market. The capabilities of WORD are examples of the features that these newer programs offer:

- Widow and orphan control (leftover words or lines)
- "Keep-together" commands for paragraphs and tables
- Full-page formatting with a variety of type sizes and styles
- Support for letter-quality daisy-wheel and thimble printers
- Support for laser-based printers
- Support for conventional typesetting equipment
- Compatibility with window-based programs
- Conversion feature for ASCII and other word processing files
- Proportional spacing and justification at both ends of lines

Graphics

In the near future, graphics programs geared to laser-based printing will supplant the pen plotter and make full-page electronic publishing—with integrated text and graphics—the standard method for preparing technical manuals and books of all types. At the present state of the art, however, affordable laser images are coarse. Use of a pen plotter and CAD software to produce original line drawings is a more satisfactory solution.

DETAILS AND PROCEDURES

This section covers the preparation of original drawings, mounting of artwork, formatting text, and the pasteup techniques that are used to make camera-ready masters. The descriptions are sufficiently detailed to provide an idea of the work that is involved. From this survey you can decide whether to purchase equipment and undertake these tasks or to hire professional help.

Preparing the Original Drawings

There is no mystery in producing professional looking drawings. Inked technical drawings, however, are different from the everyday work produced in most drafting departments.

Conventional technical illustration is done by trained people who use a mixture of tools and techniques—some from the artist's studio and some from conventional drafting practice. With computer-aided design and drafting (CAD or CADD), drawings are created with specialized software, computers, and pen plotters. The advantages of the CAD approach over traditional drafting methods are analogous to the benefits of word processing over use of a typewriter:

- Changes are easy to make
- The original designs are stored on disks
- Images can be produced quickly
- Output is uniform and of high quality

For an example of CAD system hardware and software requirements, refer to Appendix A. Regardless of the methods that are used in producing line art, quality of the final drawings is the main concern.

This book is not a primer in technical illustration but, rather, an overview of the process. The following are some planning guidelines that will ensure uniform line widths and lettering in all figures:

- Use the same pen sizes for all line art
- Use the same lettering sizes and styles
- Keep the width of drawings consistent
- Use the same quality of paper or vellum
- Use the same reduction factor when making photostats

If you follow these guidelines, the only remaining variable will be the final sizes of the drawings, and it is relatively easy to determine how much space will be required for each figure. Most of the following items are details that expand upon the guidelines. The discussion is oriented to CAD and pen plotters, but many of the same principles also apply to manual illustration methods.

Size

Make drawings larger than the intended size. Plan to prepare photostatic reductions sized to fit the area allowed for the figure in the manual. For simple drawings, make the original twice the final size. If the drawing is complex, make the original as large as necessary.

Line Width

Allow for narrowing of lines when drawings are reduced. As a general rule, use 0.5mm and 0.7mm pens on double-size drawings. Lines thinner than 0.35mm may be indistinct or disappear in reduced photostats. If you are preparing drawings for full-size reproduction, use 0.35mm and 0.5mm pens. Use the same pens for computer-generated lettering and line work.

Borders

Borders around drawings may be used or not, depending upon the visual effect desired in the finished manual. Without borders there is more flexibility in spacing figures, because the image can be moved easily when formatting pages. Differences in spacing are more obvious when the eye has a border line for reference.

Drawing Media

Prepare drawings on high-quality transparentized vellum. Use a product designed especially for pen plotters. Using cheap drafting paper will not produce clean lines.

Plotting Speed

Adjust the plotter's pen speed to produce uniform lines on the medium. Slower speeds produce thicker lines and very fast speeds cause pen skipping and broken lines.

Ink

Use plotter ink. Ink for drafting pens is not suitable for plotting pens. It may dry too fast (or too slowly) and produce erratic results.

Lettering

If using "drafting-board technology," press-down lettering, or a KROY lettering machine can produce the text and numbers for your drawings. A better alternative is to typeset the required material and use rubber cement to attach each legend or number in place. With a CAD program you can plot the final drawings in one step.

Color

In general, prepare line art in black ink on a white background. Each color requires a separate pass through the printing press, and each printing pass increases the overall cost of the manual.

Approvals

The finished drawings should be signed off before the photostats are prepared. If changes must be made in the drawings, it will be less expensive to make corrections before reproduction than after it.

Photos

Photographs are more expensive to reproduce than line drawings. Usually, a *half-tone* is required for each photo. The half-tone is an extra step in preparation and, usually the printer's responsibility. Line drawings do not require half-tones.

Although the number of photos in a manual should be kept to a minimum, the photo has its place. Plotting or drawing a complex screen image, for example, is more time-consuming than taking a photograph.

Mounting Original Drawings

Use tape to mount the original line art onto white cardboard that is at least $\frac{1}{16}$" thick. Whether the mounted drawings (usually called *boards* or *flats*) go to your printer or to a graphics house for the production of photostats, mounting is essential—unmounted art work has a short life span.

Supplies and Equipment

To prepare mounted graphics, you will need some materials and simple equipment in addition to a desk or workbench with good lighting; a light table is not required. Purchase the following items at an art or drafting supply store:

- Mounting material to fit your inked drawings
- X-acto knife (or utility knife)
- Metal straightedge with cork backing
- White artist's tape
- Eraser

Step-by-Step Instructions

> **NOTE:** Repeat steps 1–11 for each drawing and refer to Figure 4–2.

Step 1. Use an X-acto knife (or scissors) to cut away excess paper from around each drawing; use the metal straightedge as a cutting guide and leave at least ½" of paper outside the drawing area.

Step 2. Position the drawing on the white side of the mounting board.

Step 3. Use white artist's tape to adhere the sides of the drawing to the mounting board.

Step 4. Outside the area of the drawing, mark the four corners of the image area with L-shaped "tick marks" to be used as a guide when making photostats.

Step 5. Examine each mounted drawing for blemishes such as black marks or dark fibers. Use an eraser to remove the marks, or cover the blemishes with white artist's tape.

Step 6. Position a piece of tracing paper slightly smaller than the mounting board over each drawing and tape it in place at the top only.

Step 7. Cut a protective flap from brown wrapping paper that is 2" longer than your mounting board and the same width as the board.

Step 8. Position the protective flap over the tracing paper with the extra length of brown paper at the top of the mounting board and the edges even at the other three sides; fold the extra length over and behind the top edge of the board.

Step 9. Tape the folded edge of the protective flap in place on the back of the mounting board.

Step 10. Position the protective flap so that it covers the drawing and tracing paper.

Step 11. Label each mounting board (on the back) with your name, your phone number, the figure number, and the title of the user's manual.

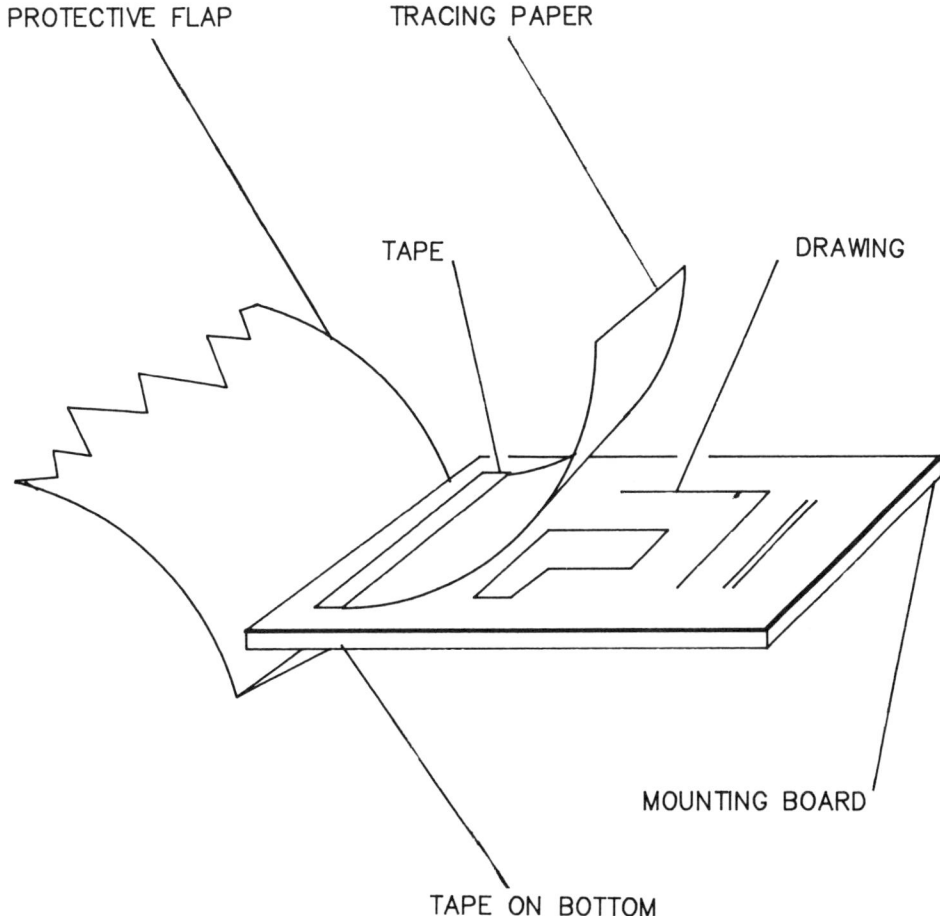

PROTECTIVE FLAP   TRACING PAPER

TAPE   DRAWING

MOUNTING BOARD

TAPE ON BOTTOM

Figure 4–2. Line drawing shows parts of mounted figure.

Handling Screen Representation

A screen representation is a special category of figure because both text and a line drawing are required. Prepare and mount a line drawing of your full-screen frame (i.e., an outline of the display). Remember to plan the screen representations so that the final sizes will be the same. Label the mounting board with non-reproducible blue pencil: "FRAME FOR FULL-SCREENS."

Prepare and mount two more line drawings, one for the top half-screen and one for the bottom half-screen. Label the mounting boards. Figure 4–3 shows the bottom half-screen frame.

Figure 4–3. Line drawing of bottom half-screen frame.

Make the necessary number of photostats of each screen frame and tape each photostat to a mounting board. At pasteup time, position the text within the frames. A figure is required for each full-screen or half-screen image.

Formatting the Manual

The following are guidelines for preparing the final text version of your user's manual. The instructions vary, depending upon whether you are preparing a reference copy for a commercial printer or using the copy to prepare camera-ready masters. If preparing masters, these guidelines apply to both "typewriter" manuals and to formatting for laser-based printers.

Spacing

For a commercial printer provide your copy, double-spaced, on 8 ½" × 11" paper. If you are going to produce a "typewriter manual" or use laser-based typography, make single-spaced copy and use the original for pasteup.

Plan for the Binding

The printer often lays out a manual, providing additional space on each page for the three-hole drilling or binding allowance. If you are doing the pasteup, provide allowance for either drilling or binding. Suitable binding techniques, in addition to three-hole drilling, are plastic- or wire-ring binding. The three-hole approach is best if you plan to revise the manual, although plastic- or wire-ring binding is less expensive.

Size of the Manual

Although IBM has popularized the half-size manual, given the choice, use an 8 ½" × 11" page size. Larger pages provide more space for the figures and the manual is not as thick. Thick manuals make people think your software is hard to use.

Margins

If using 8 ½" × 11" page, leave 1 ¼" margins on all sides of the paper. Allow space for the header at the top and the page number at the bottom. Place the header or page number not closer than ½" from the paper's edge. Margins of 1 ¼" provide ample space for binding or three-hole drilling. Narrower margins require the page image to be shifted for left- or right-hand pages. If the image is not shifted, the holes for the binding comb or the snap rings may cut into the text.

Headers and Page Numbers

The name of your user's manual should appear as a header on each page. Each page except the Title Page should have a page number. Front Matter pages are identified by lower case Roman numerals or by F–1, F–2, etc.

New Pages

Begin each chapter and table on a new page unless the table is short. Conventionally, right-hand pages are odd-numbered. If you must insert a blank page into your manual, identify the page so that the reader will not be confused. Use one of these statements consistently throughout the manual:

> **This page intentionally blank**

> **Use this page for notes**

Boldface and Underlining

Use boldface and underlining only where needed. These features are especially useful for headings and for screen or keyboard references. To a commercial printer, underlining signifies the use of italic print. A wavy underline indicates boldface.

Figure Notation

For the commercial printer, indicate the position of each figure in the left margin. Refer to the following example:

The correct way to indicate a figure in the text margin is shown here. Use a template and black ink to draw a circle or box around the figure number.

Full-Page Formatting

In preparing camera-ready masters, make your job as easy as possible by formatting pages at the word processing stage, so that they come from your daisy-wheel printer or from the laser printer in nearly finished form. Follow these guidelines:

- Leave blank space for each figure.
- Adjust the spacing so that page breaks occur where you want them to be.
- Avoid leaving a single line of a paragraph at the top or bottom of a page. Keep at least two lines together.
- Keep a section heading and the first two lines of copy following it on the same page.
- Keep a figure legend and the figure referred to on the same page or on facing pages.
- If the fit of a page is close but not quite close enough, adjust the spacing between sections (or between a figure and the text) to accomplish the fit.
- Space is a positive design element. Use space in your page design to avoid a crowded look.

Once you have produced formatted copy, you can mount pages onto pasteup boards. To complete your camera-ready masters, paste photostats into the blank spaces and make minor adjustments as necessary.

THE CAMERA-READY MASTERS

The camera-ready masters are images that look exactly like the finished pages in your manual. The masters are usually prepared on special pasteup boards or on thicker mounting boards, similar to those used for artwork. The thinner boards are less expensive.

Certain skills are required to do pasteup work. These skills are not learned by reading a few pages in a how-to book and *Where's the Manual?* is not intended as a teacher of these skills. If you have the background and experience, read this section as a review or summary of the procedures. If you lack the required skills, hire a professional pasteup artist to do the job for you.

Supplies and Equipment

You will need some supplies and a few pieces of equipment. Read this entire section to get an idea of what is involved.

Pasteup Boards

Boards are available in different sizes and most pasteup boards are larger than the finished page. For example, the Pasteze boards (T & J Graphic Art Supplies, Redwood City, CA) for 8 ½" × ll" pages measure 10" × 13". These boards are ruled in non-reproducing blue for picas, inches, and millimeters. At the corners of the image area are register marks that your printer uses to align the master during production of the negatives, which are used to make the plates from which your manual is printed.

You will need a separate pasteup for each page in your manual. Regardless of what you put on the board's surface, the procedures for preparing the masters are the same. The appearance of the printed page depends upon the quality of the original copy or figures and how accurately they are aligned on the boards.

Adhesive

"Pasting up" does not mean that you will use paste. There are three common methods for adhering copy to pasteup boards.

- Rubber cement is old-fashioned, but it works.
- Spray mounting adhesives (e.g., 3 M's Photo Mount) are much like rubber cement. Spray adhesive is excellent for large mountings, but it does not allow repositioning of your work.
- The third (and best) adhesive is a special mounting wax used for pasteup operations.

To use mounting wax, you will need either a waxing machine or a hand waxer, the latter being far less expensive than the former. Both types of waxers come with instructions. and if you follow them you should not have any problems. If you use a waxing machine, you will save a lot of time by waxing an entire sheet of copy at one time and then cutting out from the areas that you want to mount.

Cutting Paraphernalia

Use a cutting pad with a self-sealing surface. The investment of a few dollars in a professional cutting pad will make your pasteup job easier. You will also need an X-acto knife, a supply of No. 11 blades, and a steel straightedge with a cork backing. Scissors are also useful.

Drafting Pens

You will need two pen bodies and one pen tip in each of the following sizes to handle any touch-ups or miscellaneous drawing that might be required: 0.35mm, 0.5mm, 0.7mm, and 1.0mm. Both Koh-i-noor and Mars pens are excellent. Also buy a pen cleaning kit. The kit consists of a bottle of ink solvent and a plastic basket for soaking pen parts after use.

Light Box

A small light box (approximately 11" × 14") is required for accurate pasteup work. Ideally, the surface area should be slightly larger than the dimensions of the pasteup boards. A large light table is not necessary. Your light box or table may have a true straight edge that can be used as a reference for aligning the pasteup boards. If not, tape a piece of grid paper on the surface of the light table and use the grid lines for reference.

Miscellaneous Supplies

Obtain the following: a roll of masking tape, a non-reproducing blue pencil, white artist's tape, a burnisher, and an eraser. Use a T square and a 30-60-90 triangle to align your work. A pair of tweezers is useful in handling small pieces of copy. A transparent ruler that shows measurements in points, picas, millimeters, and inches is also helpful.

Laying Out Pages

You will have to decide what to fit onto each page. This is normally done on a *dummy* (working layout) before pasteup. If you are using full-page formatted text, several of these items have already been considered. If you are using galleys, note the following:

- Keep at least two lines together at the top or bottom of a page.
- Keep headings and the first two lines of the material that follows it on the same page.
- Keep a figure and its legend on the same page.
- Do not crowd the pages.
- Keep the margins and horizontal elements aligned.
- To speed up the job, work with the largest mountings that you can comfortably handle. If possible, paste up one full page at a time.
- Check often to be sure that the copy is aligned and square with the page.

Step-by-step Instructions

Whether you use word processing copy, typeset text, or laser typography to produce your user's manual, the pasteup procedures are much the same. Here is an overview:

- Make a layout template.
- Align a pasteup board over the layout template.
- Apply adhesive to the copy that you want to mount.
- Position the copy on the pasteup board.
- Check the alignment.
- Cover the copy with tracing paper, then burnish.
- Erase or tape over the blemishes.

In the material that follows, *copy* means "text," *figure* means "a sized photostat made from a mounted original of your line art," and *mount* means "to attach copy or figures with adhesive." These instructions assume that you are preparing pages in an 8 ½" × 11" format with 1 ¼" margins.

Making a Layout Template

A layout template is useful to ensure that all pages look alike. Follow the step-by-step instructions for making a template and refer to Figure 4–4.

Step 1. Place a pasteup board on your light box. Use a T square to align the board, then tape all four corners onto the light box surface with short pieces of masking tape.

Step 2. Use a non-repro blue pencil to draw margin lines with 1 ¼" inside the register marks on all four sides.

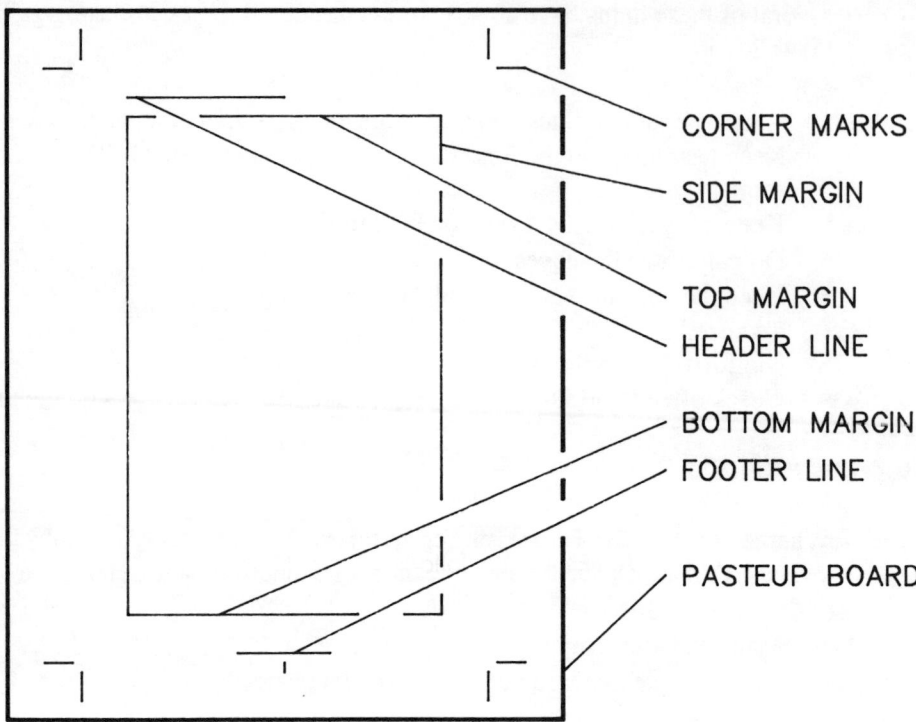

CORNER MARKS

SIDE MARGIN

TOP MARGIN
HEADER LINE

BOTTOM MARGIN
FOOTER LINE

PASTEUP BOARD

Figure 4–4. Line drawing of layout template.

Step 3. Draw two horizontal blue lines, one each at the top and bottom of the pasteup board. Each line should be ½" from the top or bottom of the image area. These lines will be used to align the headers and page numbers. If you use full-page formatted copy, position the lines to correspond with the location of the header and page numbers. Extend the margin lines to the top header line.

Step 4. Use a 0.35mm drafting pen to ink over the blue pencil lines. Usually, it is not good practice to ink over blue pencil lines; however, for the template this is not important because the image will not be reproduced.

Step 5. Place a second pasteup board on top of your layout template. Switch on the light in the light box. Align the register marks at the corners of the top pasteup board with the register marks underneath.

Step 6. Tape the top pasteup board in position, using short pieces of masking tape in each of the four corners.

Preliminary Page Layout

Step 1. Use scissors (or work on a cutting pad and use an X-acto knife) to neatly cut out the elements that you want to put on, leaving 1/16" to 1/4" of white paper all around the copy.

Step 2. Test the positioning and fit of the elements. If the copy is too long to fit on the page, carefully cut between lines and save the leftover copy for the next page. When the page looks all right, you can start pasting it up.

Simple Pasteup

As an example, consider the steps required to pasteup the header on a page. All pasteup operations are an extension of this procedure.

> **NOTE:** In the following steps, if you are using a waxing machine, wax the copy *before* cutting. If using rubber cement or spray adhesive, apply the adhesive *after* cutting.

Step 1. Apply adhesive to the back of the copy.

Step 2. Use scissors (or work on a cutting pad and use an X-acto knife) to neatly cut out the page header from your copy, leaving at least 1/16" of white paper all around the letters.

Step 3. Use a pair of tweezers or the tip of your X-acto blade to pick up the copy. Position the copy, adhesive side down, at the header position.

Step 4. Use the inked lines that show through from the layout template as a guide to align the copy. Position the copy so that the bottoms of the letters are even with the header line and the side edge is aligned with the margin line. Carefully press down the loose edges of the copy so that they stick to the pasteup board. Do not touch the text, and press down only the white edges of the paper around the lettering.

Step 5. Check to be sure that the copy is aligned, square with the layout template, and flush with the margin line. Use your T square and 30-60-90 triangle to check—don't guess.

Step 6. Place a clean piece of tracing paper over the pasteup board and use the burnisher to rub over the piece of copy just put into position. This is done to keep loose copy from getting caught under triangles, T squares, and so on, as you work on the rest of the page.

Step 7.   Clean away any wax remaining on the paper by rubbing over it gently with soft, clean tissue.

Pasting up Large Copy and Figures

There are a number of variations on the simple pasteup procedure. Large mountings, for example, are trickier to handle than small pieces of copy. Use the following procedure for full-page pasteups and figures. Handle the material with a light touch and refer to Figure 4–5.

> **NOTE:** In the following steps, if you are using a waxing machine, wax the copy *before* cutting. If using rubber cement or spray adhesive, apply the adhesive *after* cutting.

Step 1.   Apply adhesive to the back of the copy.

Step 2.   Use scissors (or work on a cutting pad and use an X-acto knife) to neatly cut out the copy or figure, leaving at least 1/4" of white paper all around it.

Step 3.   Lay a clean piece of tracing paper over the pasteup board, positioning one edge of the tracing paper just below the line where you want to place your copy.

Step 4.   Position the copy, adhesive side down, on the pasteup board. Most of the copy will lie on top of the tracing paper.

Step 5.   Use the T square and 30-60-90 triangle to be sure that the copy is aligned with the layout template and flush with the margin.

Step 6.   Slide the tracing paper down a few lines and use your T square to be sure that the copy is square with the layout template. If the copy is not aligned, lift it free from the pasteup board and start again.

Step 7.   When you are satisfied with the placement of the copy, remove the tracing paper.

Step 8.   Use your fingers to press the copy against the pasteup board. Check the alignment again.

Step 9.   Place a clean piece of tracing paper over the pasteup board and use the burnisher to rub over the copy.

Step 10.   Repeat the pasteup steps for each page of your manual.

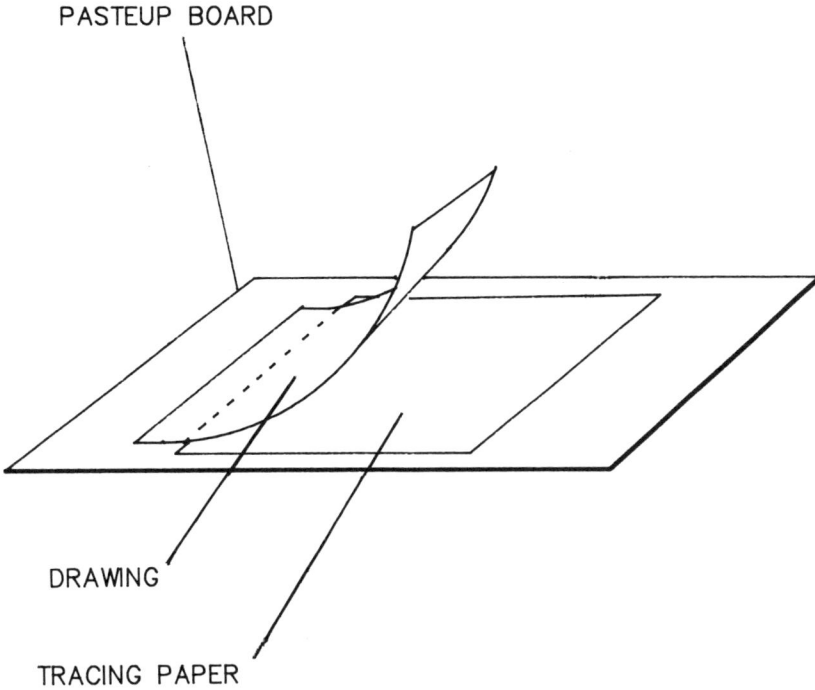

PASTEUP BOARD

DRAWING

TRACING PAPER

Figure 4-5. Line drawing shows how to paste up large copy.

PUTTING IT ALL TOGETHER

After the pasteup process is complete, there will be several other parts of the final package that must be delivered to the printer. Careful preparation of the printer's package is essential.

What the Printer Needs

The printer must know what you want the final product to look like. If you are not providing camera-ready masters, a complete package should include the following items:

- Figure legends that correspond with mounted figures and figure references in text
- Each figure mounted and covered by a protective flap
- A tracing paper overlay on each figure with special instructions listed on it
- Your name and figure number on the back of each mounted figure

- Each screen representation and the accompanying text clearly marked for full- or half-frame
- Page numbers for the Table of Contents, List of Figures, and Index assigned as the printer's responsibility
- Page layout example
- Original and photocopy of text

A much simpler package is possible if you are providing the camera-ready masters. In this case, the printer needs

- A set of camera-ready masters
- A photocopy of the user's manual
- Any special instructions

Several items appear on the first checklist that have not been discussed before. The following are guidelines for these items.

Figure Legends

The figure legend is a list of the descriptions of each figure in your user's manual. The list is needed to allow the printer or pasteup artist to position the correct legend with the appropriate picture. Refer to the following example:

FIGURE	LEGEND
1–1	Flowchart of a typical publications project. Numbers indicate major steps.
1–2	Production schedule for producing a typical user's manual. Man-loading and direct costs are indicated at the bottom of the schedule.
1–3	Project summary for a typical user's manual.
2–1	. . .

Page Layout

Your printer must know what you want in order to produce a satisfactory product. Prepare a sample page that shows margins, positions of the header and page numbers, and any other information that is important. Refer to Figure 4–6.

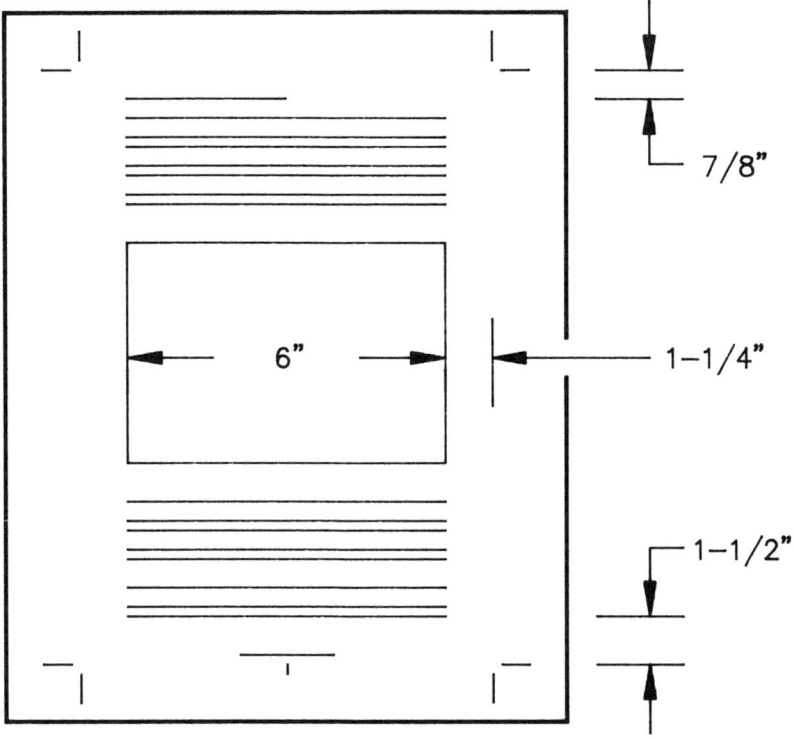

Figure 4–6. Line drawing shows page layout.

Photocopy of the Manual

Provide a clean photocopy of all material that you submit. Retain an identical copy for your files.

Delivery

Either hand-deliver your package to the printer or send it by courier. If you hand-deliver the package, be sure that you get a receipt. If you use a courier or mailing service, insure the package for several thousand dollars and request a return receipt. Regardless of your method of delivery, make a follow-up phone call to be sure that everything has arrived in good condition.

SUMMARY OF CHAPTER 4

- Decide which approach you want to take: typesetting, a "typewriter manual," or a hybrid version.
- Decide who will prepare the camera-ready masters.
- Prepare and mount the original drawings, or hire someone to do it for you.
- Obtain photostats and format the text (or obtain typeset galleys) if it is your choice to do these jobs.
- Paste up the camera-ready masters, hire someone to do this for you, or assign the responsibility to your printer.
- Put together and deliver a printer's package.

Part II

Working with Desktop Publishing Tools

5

About Electronic Publishing

Chapter 5 introduces desktop publishing and provides a short history of its development. Some common questions about training, equipment, and costs are discussed.

If you read computer magazines, you have probably seen the words "desktop publishing" or "electronic publishing," but what is desktop publishing? Who uses it? Why should you think about it? How much training would you need to use it? What equipment is necessary? Where can you buy a system? How much does it cost?

A BRIEF HISTORY

Let us start at the beginning. Electronic publishing is not new. Newspaper and magazine publishers have used computer-aided publishing tools for years. However, the electronic publishing systems that large newspapers use are very expensive and usually require a minicomputer or a mainframe with large memory and disk storage capabilities.

In the Beginning

About 1985, electronic publishing technology filtered into the world of personal computers. Early software attempts were programs like Microsoft's WORD and

WordStar 2000. These programs offered more control over page composition than was possible with a typical word processing program. Different typefaces could be used on the same page. With style sheets, the appearance of all the subheadings within a chapter could be changed in one operation, rather than one at a time. Outlining, footnote control, and generating a Table of Contents became nearly automatic operations. These were super word processing programs, but they were not real graphics programs that allowed each change to be seen immediately on the screen.

Shortly after the Beginning

Within a year, good laser printers became affordable. Not only were they fast and quiet, but they also brought graphics resolution up to 300 dots per inch (dpi), which was almost twice the resolution of a typical dot-matrix printer. During this rapid evolution, Apple's Macintosh computer, with its easy-to-use screen interface, became a testbed for dozens of graphics programs. With the graphics hardware in place and super word processing software already available, it was a short step to a true page composition program that worked on a personal computer. And so desktop publishing was born—along with a new word, *WYSIWYG* (pronounced: WIZ-E-WIG) which means "What You See Is What You Get."

By 1990, there were dozens of WYSIWYG page composition software packages that could be used on either Macintosh or PC computers. The price of some 300 dpi laser printers was under $1,000 and do-it-yourself publishing franchises appeared in store fronts across the country.

ANSWERS TO SOME COMMON QUESTIONS

Whether it is called "electronic publishing" or "desktop publishing," what really matters is that a small business or a corporate publications department can afford a WYSIWYG page composition system and with it can produce work that looks almost like typeset pages.

What Are the Main Benefits?

The main benefits are ease of use, relatively low cost, complete control over page layout, multifont capability, dramatic cost savings when compared to typeset documents, the ability to incorporate pictures directly into a document, and the ability to make changes to a manual quickly.

What about Training?

Page composition software is not difficult to learn or to use and, in general, today's programs do much more than just lay out pages. There are generalized and product-specific books about desktop publishing, and there are also do-it-yourself franchise operations in major cities where you can experiment without purchasing expensive equipment.

Many community colleges offer introductory courses in desktop publishing and major vendors of desktop publishing software have training courses. As with any new activity, however, practice will improve your skills, and working with your own system has distinct advantages.

How Much Equipment Is Needed?

Unless you are a newspaper or magazine publisher, a networked set of terminals and access to a mainframe computer with gigabytes of memory and disk space are probably beyond your budget. Most folks who use desktop publishing systems have a personal computer, monitor and laser printer—and maybe a scanner and pen plotter. You can use a workstation that is used for other tasks too, such as working up a spreadsheet, preparing a letter, or producing a mechanical drawing with CAD software. If you have a Macintosh or an AT-class computer system that is used for graphics, you probably have most of the required hardware. The following hardware and software platform was used to produce this book.

Hardware: Much of the work was done using a NOVAS 80286-based AT computer clone. A Compaq Model 40 with an 80387 math coprocessor was used for editing. A Photon MEGA graphics adapter card and a NEC Multisynch monitor were used at various resolutions (depending upon the task). Logitech's C-7 mouse was the pointing device of choice. A Canon IX-12 scanner and a QMS Kiss laser printer (both have 300 dpi resolution) were connected to a J-Laser Plus card. A Houston Instrument DMP-61 plotter produced the original pen plots.

Software: Text was produced using WordStar 3.1 or Brief, and line drawings were generated with AutoCAD. Ventura Publisher Edition (Version 2.0) and Ventura's Professional Extension were used for page composition. Scanned images were captured with White Sciences' SCANGRAB program, and screen images were recorded with Symsoft's HOTSHOT utility.

As you can see, the requirements are not too demanding. There are many people using 8088-based XT computers (with hard disks) for desktop publishing. For more information about hardware and software requirements, see Chapter 6.

What Does It Cost?

Total cost of a desktop publishing system depends upon a number of factors: How much hardware do you already have? Will you use a Macintosh or a PC? What is your budget? You can set up a basic system (hardware and software) similar to the one used to prepare this book, for $9,500 to $15,000. The technology is affordable for a small business or corporate publications department.

Is This Just Another Fad?

Advances in electronic publishing technology have been rapid during the past five years, and desktop publishing is projected to be one of the fastest growing sectors of computer activity for the next decade and beyond. Desktop publishing threatens the profitability of the typesetting industry by providing a do-it-yourself alternative. The technology is here to stay and it will become more affordable, faster, and better as it matures.

What about Quality?

The quality of 300 dpi output is marginal for applications such as annual corporate reports. However, for technical manuals, brochures, and newsletters, this quality is excellent. Higher resolutions are also available. For example, the camera-ready masters for this book were prepared at 400 × 800 dpi.

6

The PC Approach

Chapter 6 describes desktop publishing systems based on XT/AT and 80386-based computers used with Xerox's Ventura software. Figure 6–1 illustrates a typical system and provides an overview of this chapter.

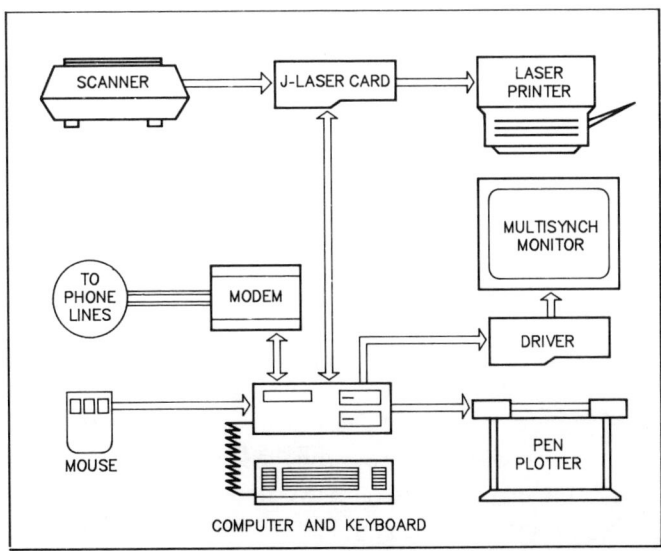

Figure 6–1. Overview of PC-based desktop publishing system.

COMPUTERS

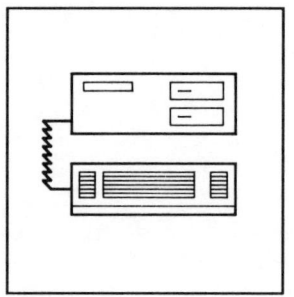

The responsiveness of your desktop publishing system depends upon the speed of your computer. Faster computers are more expensive than slower ones. Regardless of speed, however, you will need a computer with a hard disk (20 Mbyte minimum) to adequately handle fonts and pictures.

80386-Based Systems

An 80386-based Compaq computer or a 386-based clone is very fast (16–33 MHz). However, because of the speed, you may encounter compatibility problems with some software utilities and timing difficulties with some hardware. The best versions of the 386 can be set (from the keyboard) to operate at different speeds. Typically, a 386-based computer has one or two floppy drives and a 40 Mbyte hard disk. Larger disk capacities are available. Add an 80387 math coprocessor to double the speed of your system.

PS/2 Systems

IBM PS/2-80 computers are similar to the Compaq 386 but use a different (OS/2) operating system. Other PS/2 computers also use the OS/2 operating system. Presently, PS/2s are more expensive than the Compaq 386 and comparable XT or AT clones. If you own an XT or AT computer and plan to upgrade to a PS/2, note that your existing adapter cards might not work with the PS/2 hardware. In time, PS/2 systems might become an industry standard but, at present, they are not.

80286-Based (AT) Systems

An AT-class computer or clone with an 80286 microprocessor and 640 Kbytes of RAM is today's standard platform for desktop publishing and CAD applications. The best systems can be set from the keyboard to operate at different speeds. Buy a system with a hard disk and two floppy drives. One floppy drive should handle 1.2 Mbyte disks. Add an 80287 math coprocessor to double the speed of your system. Add a 3 ½" disk drive to take advantage of the newer high-density floppies that are enclosed in a protective plastic case.

8086/8088-Based (XT) Systems

You can use an IBM XT computer or clone for desktop publishing applications. You will need a 20 Mbyte hard disk and one or two 360 Kbyte floppy drives. Prices start at about $400. An 8087 math coprocessor will speed things up by a factor of two. However, even with a math coprocessor, the XT is sluggish, compared to the other computer options.

DISPLAY SYSTEMS

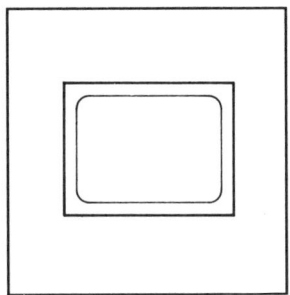

There is a trade-off between cost and screen resolution and screen size. As screen size grows and resolution increases, the cost of a monitor and graphics adapter card rises dramatically.

CGA, EGA, and Beyond

A few years ago, most affordable PC color monitors were built to the CGA standard, that is, 320 pixels × 200 lines. Graphic images on such monitors were irritating because of the "jaggies" that appeared on the screen. The CGA resolution is unacceptable for either professional graphics or desktop publishing applications. If you already have a CGA display system, you will need something better. You might be able to use a Hercules card and monochrome monitor or one of the older cards and color monitors with a resolution of 640 pixels × 400 lines. However, the less popular display systems will probably not be supported by future software.

Today's retiring display standard is an EGA card and a monitor that produces 16-color images with a screen resolution of 640 pixels × 350 lines. An EGA system is a good compromise for desktop publishing or for CAD/CAE applications. Dozens of vendors produce adapter cards and monitors to the EGA standard and dozens of software publishers sell utilities that work at this resolution. If you want an inexpensive but adequate display system, this is it.

One step beyond EGA is a new de facto standard, the VGA card and monitor that produces color images at a resolution of 640 pixels × 480 lines. And so the story continues—up to what is called "affordable good resolution," corresponding to 800 pixels × 600 lines, with 16 colors from a palette of 64. Beyond the 800 × 600 level are a number of color and monochrome display systems, most of which are beyond the scope of this book.

At the high end, however, one system stands out: the Sigma Designs LaserView. Available for the Macintosh SE and Macintosh II, as well as for PC-based systems, the LaserView provides a 1664 × 1200 monochrome display with either 15" or 19" monitors. The LaserView displays two pages at once but, you can also work on single pages at a resolution of 832 × 600.   The LaserView system was designed specifically for desktop publishing, however, there are few third-party software utilities that work at this resolution.

To get the most from a LaserView system, buy the 19" monitor. If you want to use your hardware only for editing and page composition, a large, high-resolution, monochrome display is a practical solution.

Multisynch Adapter Cards and Monitors

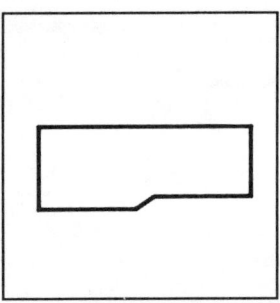

You can purchase a multisynch color adapter card that will handle all modes from CGA to 800 pixels × 600 lines. A good example is the Photon MEGA. Coupled with a NEC multisynch color monitor, this display system provides 16 colors, from a palette of 64, which makes the display suitable for CAD/CAE applications and desktop publishing. For all-around utility, a multi-synch card and monitor are excellent choices for a display system.

A multisynch system is practical if you want to capture screens from a software package running at EGA resolution and then use Ventura for page composition in the 800 × 600 mode. Other alternatives would entail card and monitor swapping or two complete computer systems—one to run the applications software and the other for desktop publishing. The dual-computer approach is a useful working configuration; however, it is much more expensive than a single-computer solution.

What You See Is What You Have to Use

On a 14" monitor, at a resolution of 800 × 600, the text on an 8 ½" × 11" page, plus standard screen menus, can be viewed in Ventura without horizontal scrolling. At this resolution, the screen is slightly larger than the printed output. You will see about two-thirds of the page length. For text that appears in 8 pt. type which you can read, you will have to squint. The alternative to squinting is not higher resolution. Either buy magnifying glasses, use 10 pt. type, or use a larger monitor.

Our Recommendation

For optimal speed, compatibility, and ease of viewing, use an AT-class computer clone with a Photon MEGA multisynch graphics adapter card and a 14" NEC multisynch monitor. If you want a faster system, use a Compaq 386 or one of the 386-based clones. For larger imagery, use a 19" multisynch display. For now, avoid the OS/2 and PS/2 environment.

OTHER HARDWARE

This section describes accessory hardware for a desktop publishing system. If you have a PostScript laser printer, the section on J-Laser cards might be of only passing interest. Pointing devices, laser printers, scanners, pen plotters, and modems are also discussed.

PostScript or J-Laser Card

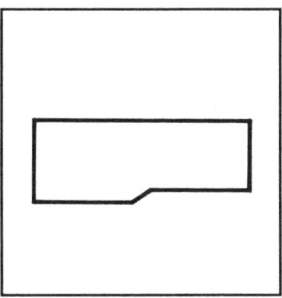

There are two schools of thought about converting the images on the screen to printed pages. One school of thought is based on the PostScript philosophy, and the other relies on the J-Laser or J-Laser Plus card. With a PostScript system, the laser printer costs more because much of the printing intelligence is built into the printer. Both IBM and Apple support the PostScript philosophy. The J-Laser approach is less popular and less expensive but prints faster.

With a J-Laser-based system, an adapter card that fits into your computer is an additional expense. Most of the printing intelligence is on the adapter card. The additional cost of a J-Laser card allows selection of a laser printer that is less expensive than one with built-in PostScript capabilities. There are three other advantages: First, the cost of a scanner controller is saved, because this is included on the J-Laser Plus card. Second, J-Laser-based systems are significantly faster than PostScript-based printing systems. Third, the J-Laser Plus card has additional memory built into the card and this memory can be accessed for a variety of purposes.

The PostScript philosophy also has some advantages. The main one is versatility. If, for example, you want to produce musical notation on your laser printer, PostScript can handle it, whereas the J-Laser card cannot. Also, if you want to send a disk to a service company for reproduction at 1200 or 2400 dpi resolution, which is equivalent to the quality of traditional typesetting, you will find more service companies that handle PostScript files than any other type.

We go along with the school of thought favoring J-Laser cards because a manual does not require super resolution and the printout is fast. If you are using a 286-based AT computer, buy the J-Laser Plus version. If you are using a 386-based computer, you will need an extended memory card, such as Intel's Above Board plus a low-cost half-slot J-Laser Card.

Pointing Device

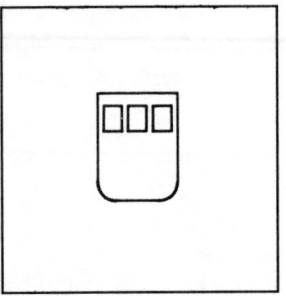

It is slow and impractical to move the cursor on your display by pressing the arrow keys on the keyboard. To work effectively, you will need a pointing device. The more common pointing devices are joy sticks, track-balls, mice, digitizing tablets, and hybrid products. Keep it simple: buy a mouse.

Mice with three buttons are more versatile than those with only two buttons. Although much of today's software is designed for one- or two-button mouse operations, the "better" programs provide for chords. Chords work with two- or three-button mice whose buttons can pressed simultaneously to accomplish different tasks. With a three-button mouse, there are eight possible button combinations (including no buttons pressed). With a two-button mouse, there are four combinations.

> **NOTE:** If you have a laptop computer your options may be limited.

There are three options for mouse-to-computer interfacing. Bus mice rely on a special adapter card that is installed in the computer. A bus mouse saves an RS-232 port but it takes up a slot in the card cage. Serial mice rely on an RS-232 communications port (Com 1 or Com 2). Other mice are designed for parallel interfacing. Avoid parallel mouse interfacing if you have only one parallel port, you will probably need it for your printer.

Serial mice are easy to connect, do not interfere with the computer's bus addressing, and are relatively inexpensive. For a cost-effective solution, try

Logitech's C-7 serial mouse. It has three buttons that can be user-programmed, and the device requires no external power supply.

Laser Printer

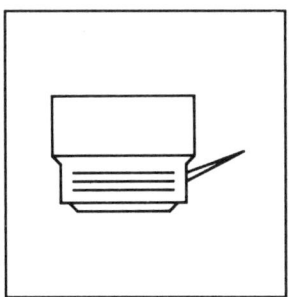

A 300 dpi laser printer is essential for serious desktop publishing. These machines offer several advantages over daisy-wheel and dot-matrix printers. First, laser printers are quiet. Second, they are fast (about 5–8 pages per minute for text). Third, the quality of the image is superior to that produced by the best impact or dot printers. Finally, you can print excellent text and graphics with the same printer.

Other printers are available. These include ink jet, dot-matrix, thermal color and electrostatic printers—forget about them. For most desktop publishing applications you will use black and white rather than color. None of the dot-matrix printers produce publications-quality output and currently, electrostatic printers are expensive. Soon, 400 and 800 dpi laser-based printers will be affordable. Higher resolution printers offer some benefits, but the main benefit will be to drive down the price of 300 dpi printers. For PostScript output, plain-paper laser printers are available at about 1000 dpi and laser printers that use special paper and processing produce images at about 2400 dpi.

For technical manuals, 300 dpi resolution is more than adequate. It is not acceptable for corporate reports or magazine publishing, but for brochures, newsletters, and manuals, it is ideal. If you need higher resolution, consider printing on a Linotronics 100 or 300 printer and you will be assured of typeset quality. For desktop applications, however, an ultra-resolution laser printer is not practical unless you can justify the cost.

Prices for 300 dpi laser printers start at about $700. The most popular PostScript-based printers, such as the H-P LaserJet or LaserJet Plus and Apple's LaserWriter, cost more. If you use a J-Laser or J-Laser Plus card, you can buy a bare-bones laser printer and save money. Check with the manufacturer to be sure that the J-Laser products are supported.

Laser-based printing technology is evolving rapidly, so read the latest desktop publishing magazines to find the best buys. As of this writing, the QMS Kiss is an excellent printer for use with the J-Laser card. It can also be connected to the computer's parallel port and used directly (bypassing the J-Laser card) for word processing and other printing assignments. QMS Kiss upgrade kits are available for changing to the PostScript approach.

Scanner

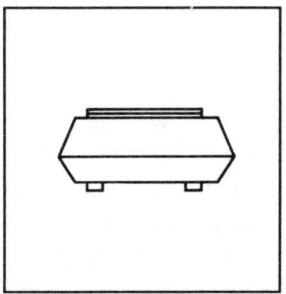

A small 300 dpi scanner is a useful peripheral for a desktop publishing system. Scanners work much like copy machines and allow you to capture into your computer system whatever image you can fit onto an 8 ½" × 11" page. Once an image is captured on a disk file, it is available for use in a document.

If you have a J-Laser or J-Laser Plus card, the interfacing intelligence for a scanner is already on the card. If you do not have a J-Laser card, you will need a separate interface card for the scanner. Both flat-bed and sheet-feed scanners are available. Select the one that best suits your needs. Flat-bed scanners can handle either single sheets or bound material such as books. Sheet-fed scanners handle only one sheet of paper at a time.

Pen Plotter

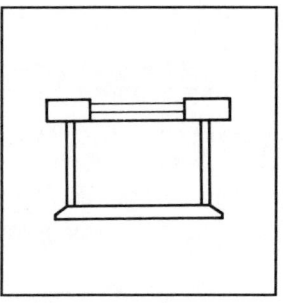

If you need to prepare precise line drawings, you will need a pen plotter. Our choice is the Houston Instrument DMP-61. The DMP-61 handles paper from ANSI A- to D-size, has a multipen attachment and boasts a resolution of 0.0005". Select the DMP-61 if you need larger drawings for other purposes in addition to desktop publishing.

Hewlett-Packard's model 7475A is a smaller A- and B-size multipen plotter with 0.001" resolution. It is suitable for desktop publishing applications and costs much less than the DMP-61.

A large plotter is not needed for electronic publishing applications, however, it provides support for CAD/CAE plotting and allows plotting of several smaller drawings at once. As a trade-off, you might be able to find a used Houston Instrument DMP-51 at a good price. The DMP-51 is a single-pen plotter with a resolution of 0.001" and it handles C- or D-size paper. Other brands are available; just be sure the machine you use has a resolution of at least 0.001".

Modem

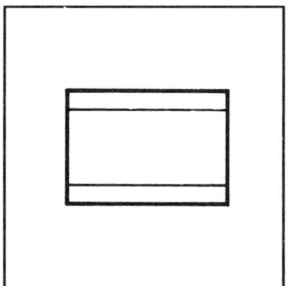

If you want to send/receive text and picture files over telephone wires, you will need a modem and communications software. Today's standards call for a Hayes-compatible modem that runs at 300 or 1200 baud. However, modems are also available for data transmission at 2400 and 9600 baud.

You will have the option of a modem card that occupies a slot in your computer's card cage—or an external modem. Often, modem cards interfere with bus addressing. They also lack indicator lights, so you cannot see whether or not the device is operating. Select an external modem.

For communications software, use Crosstalk or ProComm. If you choose a different product, it must be compatible with the Hayes modem and your computer.

SOFTWARE FOR AN MS-DOS SYSTEM

You will need specialized software for desktop publishing. The programs fall into four broad categories: page composition, word processing, graphics, and utilities.

Avoid the "do everything" desktop publishing package. Some "do everything" programs get bogged down when producing anything more demanding than a short brochure. Others ignore production of important items like the Table of Contents and Index.

Page Composition and Layout Software

Today's *de facto* standard program for page layout with an MS-DOS system is Xerox's Ventura Publisher. In the future there might be a program that has more features, better control of the page elements, and a more convenient user's interface, but for now, Ventura is the best WYSIWYG program available for preparing long technical manuals.

Ventura's main strength is its ability to accurately position (usually to 0.001") various page elements, such as frames for illustrations, margins, headers, columns, and intercolumn spacing. In addition, any number of specialty type styles can be used on the same page, and type sizes can be changed easily. Ventura utilizes both pop-up and pull-down menus. You can assign a name for each heading and subheading (there can be dozens of these in the same document), and by changing the characteristics at the menu level, all of the related headings or subheadings within a document are changed automatically; you do not have to change characteristics one at a time.

The program also includes features such as text that flows around pictures, flush left, flush right, or centering of text in columns, automatic kerning, line spacing, interline spacing (leading), and microadjustment of text (up or down) in 0.001" increments. Other features include multiple line headers and footers, automatic chapter numbering, page numbering, section and subsection numbering, and automatic generation of Tables of Contents and Indices.

Ventura's main weakness is its inability to produce other than the simplest of graphics. The program gets high marks, however, for importing and sizing scanned images, as well as PCX, CGM, IMG, DXF, HPGL, and Apple's PICT or MacPaint graphics files. Additionally, Ventura imports ASCII text files and files from all of the more popular word processors. Figure legends can be moved with pictures, and figures are numbered automatically.

Xerox also publishes the Ventura Publisher Professional Extension, an add-on utility that uses your computer's extended memory to handle long documents efficiently. Professional Extension also justifies pages vertically by adding space between figures and text, between headings and text, between paragraphs of text, or between lines of body text within paragraphs. You can control the percentage of space used in each category. There are other features also: Professional Extension generates cross references, formats matrices and complex mathematical equations, and allows you to manipulate tables easily. The following equations were produced with Professional Extension.

$$F(x) = \frac{1}{\sigma\sqrt{2\pi}} \int_{-inf}^{(x-u)/\sigma} e^{-u^2/2} \, \sigma \, du$$

$$\sum_{n=0}^{\infty} \left\{ \left(\frac{n+k}{n} \right) \right\}^{-1}$$

We recommend Ventura Publisher as an excellent page composition and layout program. If you want more information, refer to the trade magazines or to any of the Ventura-specific tutorials available at bookstores.

Word Processing Software

Word processors are better than page composition programs for tasks such as text entry, block moves, and general letter writing. Most of the popular word processing programs generate files that can be imported into page composition programs. You can use any of the following word processing programs with Ventura: Displaywrite III and IV, Microsoft's WORD, Multimate, Word Perfect, WordStar, WordStar 2000, Lotus Manuscript, Xerox Writer, and any program that generates a standard ASCII file.

A separate word processing program makes it easy to exchange information. If several people are working on a document and one of them is more familiar with WordStar, that user can run WordStar while others are using WORD or Word Perfect. When collecting all of the input into the page layout program, you will have no problems (with Ventura) because the input from several word processing programs can be mixed and the final product will be uniform.

As a practical consideration, continue using the word processor that you already have, or try WordStar (Version 3) or Word Perfect. Do not be misled by claims that word processing software is the same as desktop publishing software. Although you can use Microsoft's WORD, Word Perfect (Version 5) or WordStar 2000 for a certain level of page composition, in a PC environment these programs are not as easy to use or as effective as a top-of-the-line page composition and layout program.

Graphics Software

For professional looking line drawings, use a good vector-based 2-D drawing package. You can spend a few hundred dollars for a program such as Prodesign II, or a few thousand dollars for a super drafting program such as AutoCAD or FastCad. You do not need a 3-D drafting package. Occasionally, you might want to produce an isometric drawing, but for software manuals, this would be an unusual event.

Look for a program that is easy to learn and use. It should allow you to size and place text or dimensions anywhere on the drawing. If the program handles multiple layers, that is a plus. Your vector-based graphics program should output files in DXF format to ensure compatibility with other graphics software. AutoCAD is the most popular and fully-featured of today's programs. The latest 3-D release (Version 10) is not necessary. Excellent work can be done with the older versions of AutoCAD. You may be able to obtain an older version, such as 2.15 or 2.5, from a dealer (or a newspaper ad) at discount prices. When vector-based images are enlarged or reduced the lines remain crisp and clear, but such programs are not especially good for freehand work.

By the time this book is printed, one or more of the Cricket software packages should be available for use with Ventura. Cricket Draw has proven itself as an excellent Macintosh program and it should be equally useful on the MS-DOS platform. Other freehand drawing packages that should give good results include Micrografx's Designer and Adobe's Illustrator.

For freehand drawing or sketches, a raster-based program is convenient but not necessary. Be sure the program generates files in the PCX or IMG format. Try Dr. Halo or PC-Paintbrush. As an alternative to a paint program, you can make a freehand sketch and scan the image into your system. Also consider clip art as a source of pictures. These collections contain previously sketched objects that range from people to trees to automobiles. You can purchase clip art on disks, but it is less expensive to prepare it yourself with a scanner and hardcopy clip art.

For business graphics, use a program developed specifically for that task. Microsoft Chart and Harvard Business Graphics are good examples. For producing graphs of engineering or scientific data, either prepare the drawing with AutoCAD, or use a specialty program such as Jandel's Sigma Plot or Tech-Graph-Pad from Binary Engineering.

Utility Software

Four utility software packages are recommended for use in preparing software manuals: The first is HOTSHOT, a program designed to capture and store images directly from monitor to disk. The second program, SCANGRAB, works with a J-Laser card and stores scanned images in PCX-compatible disk files. The third utility is Brief, an excellent ASCII file editor, and the last is VP-to-the Max, a spelling checker, thesaurus, dictionary, and search-and-replace utility that works seamlessly with Ventura.

HOTSHOT is a memory-resident utility program. It is loaded into your computer's random access memory (RAM) and when you want to capture a screen image you press a "hot key" to activate the program. A pop-up menu appears and you specify the filename you want to use. Press: **ENTER** and the image is saved for later processing. Several postprocessing options are available: you can generate gray-scaled images, make the image larger or smaller, and produce inverse (black image on white background) graphics. The program works with CGA, EGA, VGA, ATT 6300, and Hercules graphics monitors.

SCANGRAB is a link between a scanner and disk-based storage facilities. Without a utility like SCANGRAB, you will need a raster-based program such as Dr. Halo or PC-Paintbrush if you want to capture scanned imagery via the J-Laser board. SCANGRAB works at the DOS command level.

First, install the program. Then, at the C-prompt, type: SGRAB **ENTER**. A menu appears from which you select **PICTURE, DISK,** or **LINE. PICTURE** is used for continuously toned images such as photos. **LINE** represents sketches or other black and white artwork, and **DISK** refers to saved images. After you make your selection, the image is either scanned onto the screen or an image file is recalled from disk and displayed on your screen. You have the option to crop or cut off parts of the displayed image. Next, you can either PRINT the image or SAVE to a disk file. SCANGRAB generates MAT files that are PCX compatible. The MAT files can be used directly in Ventura or imported into other raster-based programs that recognize the PCX file format.

BRIEF is an ASCII file editor that was designed for programmers. Multiple windows can be opened on the screen and a different file can be displayed in each window. Blocks of text can be moved from window to window (or file to file). In many ways, Brief has the advanced features you might expect (but do not find in most word processing programs). The program supports user-defined macro functions, can be accessed from the DOS prompt anywhere within your computer's file structure, and is especially useful for editing or indexing Ventura text files. If you use a mouse with Brief, it is easy to scroll within a file and you can assign macros to different buttons for marking text and reformatting paragraphs.

VP-TO-THE-MAX is a third-party program that adds two missing functions to Ventura: spell checking, and search and replace. The search-and-replace function automatically ignores the formatting commands that appear in Ventura's text files. The utility has a built-in thesaurus and dictionary. You can add new words to the dictionary. It is easy to install VP-to-the-Max and once installed, it operates from a pull-down menu and pop-up windows, exactly like any other Ventura menu selection.

DIFFERENT TYPE STYLES

Different type styles can be downloaded into Ventura. Although the Ventura versions of Times (Dutch) or Helvetica (Swiss) are adequate for most technical manuals, it is often convenient to have other fonts for brochures, special projects, or newsletters. Bitstream Fontware is a source of fonts that can be stored on disk and used as needed. Pictures and fonts (especially the larger point sizes) occupy a lot of disk space. A large font can occupy over 1 Mbyte of storage space, depending upon the thickness of the letters and the type style.

Bitstream Cooper Black

Broadway®

Cloister Black®

University Roman

Brush Script®

Blippo Black®

Hobo®

Windsor®

Swiss Compressed

Swiss Extra Compressed

Exotic Demi-Bold

Exotic Bold

ITC Zapf Chancery®
Medium Italic

Coronet Bold

Clarendon

Clarendon Bold

Figure 6–2. Bitstream font samples.

It is good practice to store unused fonts and pictures on floppy disks. Figure 6–2 shows a sampling of fonts from Bitstream.

RESOURCES

New products are introduced every day and prices change continuously. This book cannot tell you what specific products you should buy. However, there is an easy way to lead you toward that information. Table 6–1 and 6–2 outline hardware and software resources.

Equipment and Information Resources

Go to the library or to bookstores and look at the current issues of the following magazines: *Byte, Computer Graphics World, Macworld, PC World, Publish,* and

Personal Publishing. If you can find only three of these magazines, you will probably find a half-dozen articles and/or reviews of products that are especially designed for desktop publishing applications. You will find not only the latest specifications and prices, but also the names, addresses, and phone numbers of the manufacturers. Read the advertisements too. You might want to buy directly from the manufacturer, distributor, or a discount computer hardware and/or software company.

Table 6–1. Hardware Resources

Hardware	Manufacturer's Address	Notes
Computers, EGA Cards, Monitors	Computrade 780 Trimble Rd., Ste. 605, San Jose, CA 95131	NOVAS XT/AT/386/486 clones. 99% IBM /Compaq compatible. Also graphics adapter cards, monitors, and upgrade components.
Graphics Card	Hercules Computer Technology, Inc. 2550 9th St. Berkeley, CA 94710	Hercules graphics adapter card.
Graphics Card (PCG)	Personal Computer Graphics Corp. 5819 Uplander Way Culver City, CA 90230	Multisynch half-slot graphics cards.
Monitor (Multisynch)	NEC Home Electronics (U.S.A.), Inc. 1255 Michael Dr. Wood Dale, IL 60191	Multisynch color monitors.
Pointing Device	Logitech, Inc. 6505 Kaiser Dr. Fremont, CA 94555	Logitech C–7, bus, and high-resolution mice.
J-Laser Card	TallTree Systems, Inc. 2585 E. Bayshore Rd. Palo Alto, CA 94303	J-Laser and J-Laser Plus cards.

Table 6–1. Hardware Resources (*Continued*)

Hardware	Manufacturer's Address	Notes
Laser Printer	The Laser Connection P.O. Box 850296 Mobile, AL 36685	QMS Kiss (and many other models). Laser printers and adapter/conversion kits.
Modem	Hayes Microcomputer Products, Inc. 5923 Peachtree Indust. Blvd. Norcross, GA 30092	Hayes Smartmodem 300/1200/2400/9600 Baud.
Scanner	Canon (U.S.A.) Inc. One Canon Plaza Lake Success, NY 11042	Stand-alone scanners and interfacing cards.
Plotter (HI)	Houston Instrument 8500 Cameron Rd. Austin, TX 78753	Precision plotters: Model DMP-51 (C- to D-size). Model DMP-61 (A- to D-size).
Plotter (H-P)	Hewlett-Packard Corp. 16399 W. Bernardo Dr. San Diego, CA 92127	Precision plotters: Model 7575 (A- to B-size).

Table 6–2. Software Resources

Software	Manufacturer's Address	Notes
AutoCAD	Autodesk, Inc. 2320 Marinship Way Sausalito, CA 94965	Vector-based computer-aided design and drafting (CADD). Version 10 available for PC/XT/AT/PS-2/386, Sun, and Macintosh.

Table 6–2. Software Resources (*Continued*)

Software	Manufacturer's Address	Notes
Brief	Solution Systems 541 Main St., Suite 410 S. Weymouth, MA 02190	ASCII editing program.
Crosstalk	Microstuf, Inc. 1845 Exchange, Ste. 205 Atlanta, GA 30339	Professional data communications software.
Dr. Halo	IMSI 1299 Fourth St. San Rafael, CA 94901	Various raster-based (Dr. Halo) and vector-based graphics programs, plus utilities.
Fontware	Bitstream, Inc. Athenaeum House 215 First St. Cambridge, MA 02142	Type fonts for Ventura and other page composition programs.
HOTSHOT	Symsoft, Inc. 444 First St. Los Altos, CA 94022	Screen capture utility.
PC-Paintbrush	Z-Soft Corp. 1950 Spectrum Circle Ste. A495 Marietta, GA 30067	Raster-based graphics (PCX).
ProComm	Datastorm Technologies, Inc. P.O. Box 1471 Columbia, MO 65205	Professional data communications software.
Prodesign II	American Small Business Computers, Inc. 118 S. Mill St. Prior, OK 74316	Low-cost vector-based computer-aided design (CAD) software. Also 3-D software.

Table 6–2. Software Resources (*Continued*)

Software	Manufacturer's Address	Notes
SCANGRAB	White Sciences, Inc. P.O. Box 338 Branson, MO 65616	Scanner capture utility for use with J-Laser card. Also vector-based publishing software.
Ventura	Xerox Corp. 101 Continental Blvd. El Segundo, CA 90245	Ventura Publisher page composition and layout software (Version 2.0).
VP-to-the-Max	Aristocad, Inc. 1650 Centre Pointe Drive Milpitas, CA 95035	Ventura utility: search and replace, spelling checker, thesaurus, and dictionary.
WordStar	MicroPro International Corp. 33 San Pablo Ave. San Rafael, CA 94903	One of the oldest tried-and-true word processing programs.

ABOUT THE GRAPHICS IN THIS CHAPTER

The overview figure at the beginning of this chapter (Figure 6–1) was generated with AutoCAD software and plotted on a Houston Instrument DMP-61 pen plotter. The original AutoCAD file was renamed and SAVEd. After the arrows and legends were removed, the drawing was plotted a second time to produce a single picture containing all of the icons. Finally, using Ventura, frames were created and positioned where needed on the pages. To produce the camera-ready masters, icons were cut from the plot and pasted up inside the appropriate frames. The Bitstream font examples (Figure 6–2) were provided by Bitstream.

7

Special Ventura Applications

The applications in Chapter 7 are specific to the PC and Ventura environment; however, much of what is covered also applies to other systems. For the following applications, you must know how to use Ventura and should have available a desktop publishing system similar to the one described in Chapter 6.

RENAMING STYLE SHEETS

If you are working on several projects (e.g., a brochure, newsletter, and manual) make a different style sheet for each project. For example, for a technical manual, start with Ventura's style sheet named < &TDOC-P1.STY>. SAVE the original style sheet under a new name and make changes to the renamed version. At the File pull-down menu, Select: **Save As New Style**. SAVE the style sheet as < ABC-1.STY> and modify the renamed style sheet to suit your manual. You can make variations such as < ABC-2.STY> and < ABC-3.STY> for other manuals. If you are preparing a newsletter, start with Ventura's < &NEWS-P3.STY>. For a brochure, try < &BRO-P3.STY>. Remember, to SAVE the original style sheet under a new name and make changes to the renamed version. Otherwise, you will lose the original style sheet.

PACKAGING AND PAGE LAYOUT

The thickness of a manual has a psychological effect on the user. The thicker the manual, the more intimidating it is. Pay attention to the estimated page count of your manual. Sometimes you can control the thickness of a manual by selecting a different package size. Software users' manuals come in two basic sizes: the standard minibinder with 8 ½" × 5 ½" (or 6") pages. A larger package, with 8 ½" × 11" pages, fits into a three-ring loose-leaf binder. In addition, plastic- or wire-ring bindings are sometimes used to reduce packaging costs.

Package Selection

If your manual is relatively short, use a three-ring minibinder. If your manual is over 100 pages in length, consider an 8 ½" × 11" binder. A slip box for the binder keeps your manual square with other books and manuals on a bookshelf.

It is easy to upgrade or maintain a manual in the three-ring binder format. It is impractical to upgrade a plastic-ring or wire-bound manual. However, the wire-bound manual has its place. For short documents (30–60 pages) such as "Getting Started" manuals, you can use wire-ring binding because it is more cost-effective to reprint the entire manual than to make changes and send out correction lists. Print wire-bound manuals in small numbers (under 500 at a time).

Margins and Register Marks

For an 8 ½" × 11" manual, use 1 ¼" margins on the left and right sides of all pages. There is no need to offset the text because the margins are wide enough to allow three ⁵⁄₁₆" holes for the binding rings or to carry the plastic- or wire-ring binding. Locate a printing shop that can handle the finished 8 ½" × 11" sheets without register marks on the camera-ready masters. Otherwise, you will have to paste up each page on flats or mounting boards.

For a 5 ½" (or 6") × 8 ½" page format, you must have register marks on each page or you will be inviting trouble from the printing shop. The reason is simple. You are providing the printing shop with 8 ½" × 11" sheets, and unless you specify what you want, the printer will not know how, or where, to cut the finished pages. For a page 6" wide, use a ¾" margin on both the left and right sides. This allows enough space to punch ⁵⁄₁₆" holes without punching through the text. For a page that is 5 ½" in width, use a ⅝" margin on the binding side and ⅜" on the unbound (outer) margin. This allows enough space for ⁵⁄₁₆" holes without punching through the text, but you will need to offset the text. Remember, the outer margin on a left-hand page is on the left, and for a right-hand page, the outer margin is on the right. Make a style sheet with three sets of register marks. Refer to Figure 7–1.

Figure 7–1. Register marks for minimanuals.

To create the register marks, Select Ventura's **Graphics Icon**, then Select the **Line Icon**. At the top of the screen, Select the **Graphic** pull-down menu and from the menu, Select: **Grid Settings**. Set the vertical and horizontal grid to 0.05" and select the **Grid Snap** (ON) option. Draw the lines where you want them. It may take some trial and error to get exactly the result you want but once you have the register marks positioned correctly, they will repeat automatically on every page and will not need to be changed again.

Filler (Blank) Pages

It is important that all chapters start on an odd-numbered page and end on an even-numbered page. Odd-numbered pages are those on the right-hand side when a book or manual is open. For the sake of the user, do not invent a manual with odd-numbered pages on the left.

If a chapter ends on an odd-numbered page, insert a filler page to make things work out correctly. This is especially important if you are using index tabs to separate sections of the manual. If the pagination is not correct, the last page of the chapter (or the first page of the following chapter) will end up on the wrong side of the index tab. In professionally prepared manuals, the filler pages are identified. Often you will see the following message in the middle of a filler page:

> **This page intentionally blank.**

A lot of people make jokes about this. However, you must identify the filler pages or put your trust in the printing shop. We use a variation (at the top of the page) that makes the blank page useful:

Use this page for notes.

Space for Figures

In the early stages of writing, it is convenient to ignore the figures in a document. However, you should leave space for figures or you will never have a good idea of your document's length. About 15 carriage returns provide enough space in Ventura for a figure that is 3 ¼" high. If necessary, include a brief figure legend, centered under the space.

Headers and Footers

Headers should not be confused with headings or headlines. Headers and footers consist of the uppermost and lowermost text on each page. You have several choices about the information and placement of the information in the header or footer. The more obvious choices include

- Name of the manual
- Chapter name
- Page and section numbers
- Your company name

Think of your finished manual as if it were open in front of you The inside headers and footers (those nearest the binding) are used for less important information. The outside headers and footers are used for more important items, such as the page numbers and chapter titles. Notice that the headers and footers alternate in position, from binding margin to outer margin, depending upon whether the page is odd- or even-numbered. Remember: *Right-hand pages are odd-numbered.*

Place a copyright mark (©) and the copyright holder's name on each page. Because the copyright information is relatively less important, position it toward the binding margin or center it in the footer.

The Ventura **Headers & Footers** selection is part of the **Page** pull-down menu. Move the cursor to **Page** then Select: **Headers & Footers** then **CLICK**. Refer to Figure 7–2.

Making Tab Stops Work for You

To line up columns or indentations on a page, use tab stops. Adding spaces does not always work. In the next example, spaces were used to align the material.

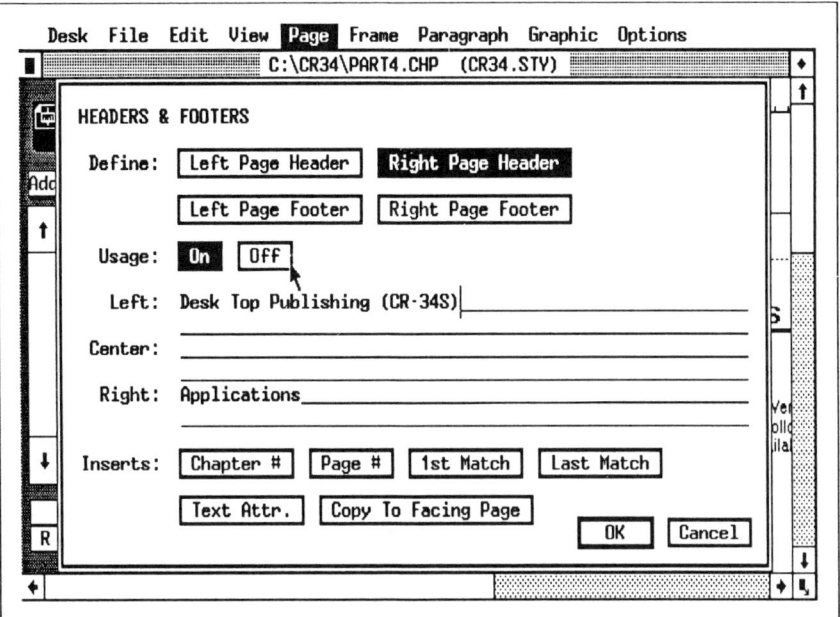

Figure 7–2. Ventura's HEADERS & FOOTERS menu.

Step 7.   Move the cursor to the box and CLICK.
        Observe: The box is filled with crosshatching.
        To delete crosshatching, move the cursor to
        the crosshatched area and CLICK

The same text, aligned with tabs, produces professional-looking results. Refer to the following example.

Step 7.   Move the cursor to the box and CLICK.
       Observe: The box is filled with crosshatching.
       To delete crosshatching, move the cursor to
       the crosshatched area and CLICK

In both of the preceding examples, the alignment of the text looks correct on the screen, but when it is printed, the misalignment shows up. Misalignment is caused by the different number of characters in each line and by slight differences between the screen display and the printed output. For manuals with step-by-step instructions, create a **Step List Tag** with a tab stop to align the text in the step. Outdent and boldface the word "Step" and the number. Use the tab to position lines of text.

Ventura's Professional Extension

Certain formatting tasks are difficult to accomplish without special tools. Ventura's Professional Extension makes it easy to do the following jobs:

- Justify columns vertically so that multiple columns are even at the bottom of a page.
- Justify pages vertically so that page lengths are equal from one page to the next.
- Create mathematical expressions. Refer to the examples in Chapter 6.
- Manipulate tables (e.g., add or delete rows and columns, add text to a single cell in the table, merge several columns, extend headings across several columns, and so forth).

A CRASH COURSE IN TYPOGRAPHY

There are hundreds of fonts available for desktop publishing systems. You can download fonts into your system and print almost any type style or size that you choose. The type style that you select for the body of your manual is called *body text*. The small type on this and other pages of this book is an example of body text in Ventura's Dutch Normal type style.

Points

Type size is usually designated in *points*. There are 72 points (abbreviated pt. or pts.) per inch. Headings and headlines are usually set in type that is larger than the body text. The heading above this subsection is set in 12 pt. Swiss Bold.

Leading

Leading is the space between lines of type. Normally, leading is 2 pts. larger than the type size. For example: use 10 pt. type on 12 pt. leading. Unless you have a strong background in typography, use Ventura's default values. For the body text of this book, the type is 11 pt. and leading is 13 pt.

Justification

Horizontal justification is the adjustment of word and letter spacing to make lines of type equal in length. This book is set with justified type (sometimes called *flush right* and *flush left*). Another common alignment is called *ragged right*.

Vertical justification is accomplished by adding space before and/or after figures, headings, paragraphs of text, or even lines of text to make adjacent columns equal in length or to make copy on all pages the same length.

Avoiding Too Many Type Styles

There are two basic fonts that work well for technical manuals: one is Helvetica and the other is Times. Ventura refers to these as Swiss and Dutch, respectively. As a rule of thumb, use the same type style for headings as for body text—or you can use Swiss for body text and Dutch for headings, or vice versa, but do not use more than two type styles.

A page set in 10 pt. Dutch (Times) contains more characters than the same page set in 10 pt. Swiss (Helvetica). If you look carefully at the laser-printed output, the Swiss font stands out clearly on the page and, because it also appears larger, it is easier to read than Dutch. On the other side of the coin, Times comes from the London Times newspaper. After exhaustive study, British typographers found that, for long columns of print, Times Roman was easier to read than anything else. Refer to the following examples and make your own judgment.

There are two basic fonts that work well for technical manuals: one is Helvetica and the other is Times. Ventura refers to these as Swiss and Dutch, respectively. As a rule of thumb, use the same type style for headings as for body text—or you can use Swiss for body text and Dutch for headings, or vice versa, but do not use more than two type styles.

A page set in 10 pt. Dutch (Times) contains more characters than the same page set in 10 pt. Swiss (Helvetica). If you look carefully at the laser-printed output, the Swiss font stands out clearly on the page and, because it also appears larger, it is easier to read than Dutch. On the other side of the coin, Times comes from the London Times newspaper. After exhaustive study, British typographers found that, for

10 pt. Helvetica (Swiss)

There are two basic fonts that work well for technical manuals: one is Helvetica and the other is Times. Ventura refers to these as Swiss and Dutch, respectively. As a rule of thumb, use the same type style for headings as for body text—or you can use Swiss for body text and Dutch for headings, or vice versa, but do not use more than two type styles.

A page set in 10 pt. Dutch (Times) contains more characters than the same page set in 10 pt. Swiss (Helvetica). If you look carefully at the laser-printed output, the Swiss font stands out clearly on the page and, because it also appears larger, it is easier to read than Dutch. On the other side of the coin, Times comes from the London Times newspaper. After exhaustive study, British typographers found that, for long columns of print, Times Roman was easier to read than anything else. Refer to the following

10 pt. Times (Dutch).

Figure 7–3. A comparison of two 10 pt. type styles.

> # Chapter Heading (18 pt. Bold, Swiss).
>
> ## MAJOR HEADING (13 PT. BOLD, SWISS).
>
> ## Minor Heading (12 pt. Bold, Swiss).
>
> ### *Minor Subheading (11 pt. Bold, Italics, Swiss).*
>
> Body Text (11 pt. Normal, Dutch).

Figure 7–4. Different types of headings used in this book.

Headings

There are several ways to make a heading or headline stand out:

- Use a different (or larger) typeface.
- Indent or center the heading on the page.
- Underline the heading or use all capitals.
- Use serial numbering.

As you read this book, you will notice some of these types of headings. Refer to Figure 7–4.

STORING AND ARCHIVING FILES

Because hard disk space is limited, store your projects on floppy disks. Make a working directory containing your current Ventura project files and another directory for pictures. When you switch from one project to another, copy the contents of both directories onto floppy disks.

Storing Ventura Files

Name the style sheet to correspond to the name of your manual (e.g., < ABC.STY>). Name each of Ventura's chapter files < xxx.CHP>, making "xxx" the same as the chapter name of your manual. Name each word processing file with the same name as its chapter (for example, < xxx.WS>). To copy a project onto floppy disks, Type: COPY <xxx.*> and everything will be transferred at once. Remember to copy the style sheet also. Refer to the following example:

Step 1. (At the C-prompt) Make a working directory named WORK.

Step 2. Load your word processing files into WORK. (For the rest of this example, we will assume that one of your word processing files is named < INTRO.WS>).

Step 3. Start Ventura and select: **File, Open Chapter**. A pop-up menu appears with whatever working directory you were using last.

Step 4. (At: **Directory**) Use **DEL** to remove the existing directory name. For example, if you are using the TYPESET directory, you will start with: C:\TYPESET*.CHP. After you delete TYPESET, you will end up with: C:*.CHP.

Step 5. Type: WORK **ENTER**. You will end up with: C:\WORK*.CHP.

Step 6. (At: **Selection**) Type the name of the first chapter of your manual. For example, Type: INTRO.CHP ENTER. Refer to Figure 7–5:

Step 7. Select: **File, Load Text/Picture, Text, WordStar** (or whatever word processing program you are using) **ENTER**.

Step 8. From the pop-up menu, Select: INTRO.WS **ENTER** Observe: The file loads and appears on the screen.

Step 9. Rename your existing style sheet (for example): ABC.STY.

Step 10. Use the: **File, Save As** option and at: **Selection**, Type: INTRO.CHP **ENTER**.

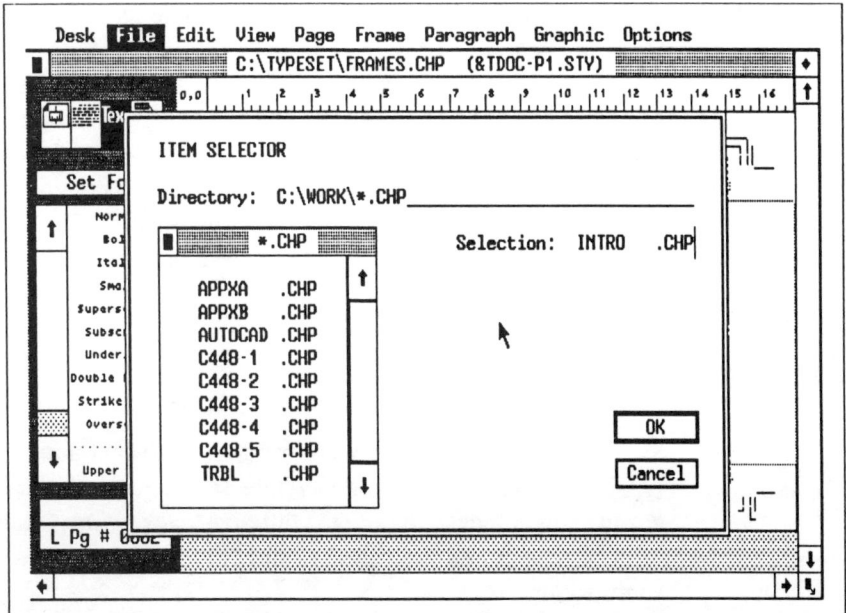

Figure 7–5. Ventura's Chapter directory screen.

Step 11. Exit Ventura and change to the WORK directory (CD\WORK **ENTER**). Call up the directory (DIR **ENTER**). On the screen, you will see all of the Ventura files for INTRO: < xxx.CIF>, <xxx.GEN>, <xxx.WS>, <xxx.CHP>, < xxx.CAP>, and < xxx.VGR>.

Step 12. Put a formatted floppy disk into drive A and Type: COPY INTRO.* A: **ENTER**. Then copy the style sheet: COPY ABC.STY A: **ENTER**.

That is all there is to it. For each new chapter, make the prefix file names (the characters before the dot) for that chapter the same. If, at a later time, you need to work on only one chapter, you can load all of the Ventura files for that chapter into the WORK directory without hunting for files.   Ventura's **Copy All** command performs a similar function. Because you are using a discrete style sheet < ABC.STY> for the manual, it is an easy matter to keep the format consistent.

Storing Picture Files

Pictures take up an immense amount of disk space. For example, a captured screen in PCX format, occupies 1–30 Kbytes and a scanned photo may occupy over 100 Kbytes. Within Ventura, PCX files are converted to IMG files and the IMG files occupy additional space. Because pictures are so space hungry, put them into a separate directory. For example, make a directory called PICTURES or PIX and use that directory for all of the pictures in your chapter or project. When it is time to put your project into storage, copy the contents of the directory onto floppy disks. Save the picture disks with your disks from the WORK directory.

Archiving utilities are special programs that compress files by about 50 percent (the range is 30–90 percent, depending upon the makeup of the file's contents). Thus, a PCX picture file that occupies 30 Kbytes can be stored in about 15 Kbytes of disk space. When the file is "uncrunched" it regains its original size. Several archiving utilities are available via modem from SHAREWARE. Public domain and low-cost programs are available from electronic bulletin boards.

CAPTURING SCREENS

Symsoft's HOTSHOT software captures both text and graphics screens at CGA, EGA VGA, ATT 6300, and Hercules resolutions. You can manipulate, crop, and change from black-on-white to white-on-black. Gray-scaled images are produced in PCX format and are accessed directly by Ventura and a number of other page composition programs.

Here is how the program works (we will assume that HOTSHOT lives in a directory named HS):

Step 1. At the C-prompt, Type: CD\HS **ENTER**.

Step 2. (If you have an EGA monitor) Type: GRAB 4 **ENTER**. For each graphics card, you will type a different number. (To capture text screens) Type: HS **ENTER**.

Step 3. (To return to the root directory) Type: CD\ **ENTER**.

Load and run the applications software of your choice. When you want to capture a screen, follow these steps:

Step 1. Press simultaneously: **ALT–P.** On the screen you will see a pop-up menu that requests a filename to which you will SAVE the captured screen.

> **NOTE**: In the next step, use of the "F" before "TEST" makes it easy to batch-process the files when gray-scaling.

Step 2. (To save the file onto the C-drive, in the PICTURES directory, under the name < TEST1> Type: C:\PICTURES\FTEST1 **ENTER**. The file extension (.PCX) is automatically added.

Converting Captured Screens

You can switch to different applications programs and use HOTSHOT to capture both text and graphics screens. To convert the captured screens to gray-scaled images, follow these steps:

Step 1. Exit the applications program and return to the root directory.

Step 2. (At the C-prompt) Type: CD\HS **ENTER**. Type: CVRT **ENTER**. A pop-up menu appears requesting the file name(s) to convert.

> **CAUTION**: In the next step, the "F" is important. If you leave it out and use "*.*" instead, the program will convert (already converted) files over and over again—until your hard disk is full.

Step 3.   Type: C:\PICTURES\F* **ENTER**. The file extension (.PCX) is automatically added.

Get up and stretch while the file conversion proceeds. Each <Fxxx.PCX> file is gray-scaled and renamed <GFxxx.PCX>. Both the original and the gray-scaled file are now in the PICTURES directory. At this point, you are ready to use the <GFxxx.PCX> files within Ventura.

Batch-Printing Your Pictures in Ventura

If you have a multichapter manual and many pictures that are not yet in the right sequence, you may find it easier to print all the pictures at once rather than to incorporate them electronically into the chapter files. Later on, you can include the pictures (electronically) or you can paste up the pictures into the camera-ready master. Figure 7–6 is one of several layouts that reside in a Ventura chapter called: FRAMES. To create a FRAMES chapter, follow these steps:

Step 1.   Open Ventura and create a new chapter. Name it: < FRAMES.CHP>.

Step 2.   Create two frames per page on several consecutive pages. Each frame measures 3 ¼" high × 4 ½" wide.

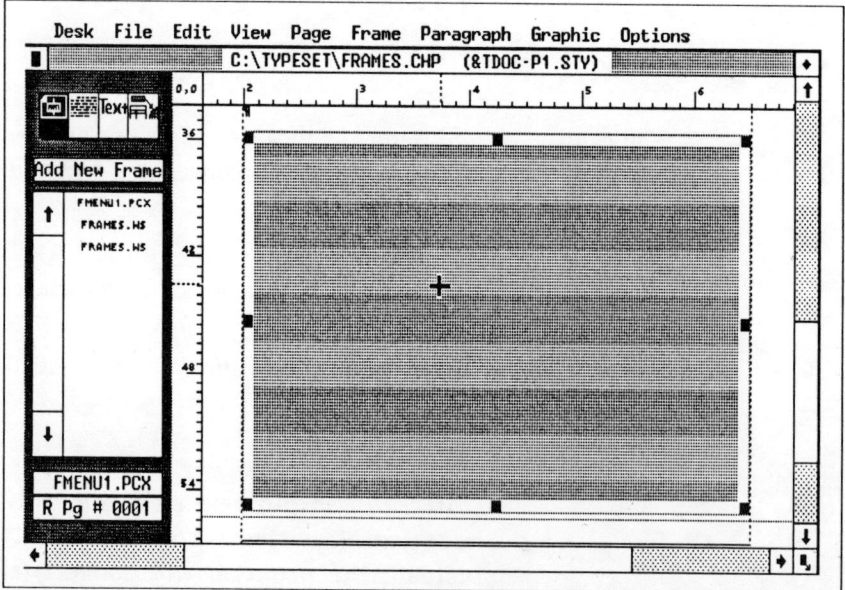

Figure 7–6. Ventura screen, FRAMES.

Step 3. For each frame, Select: **Frame, Ruling Box Around**. Set: Height of Line 1 to 0.010".

Step 4. For each frame, Select: **Frame, Margins & Columns.** Set: Margins (on all four sides) to 0.10".

Step 5. Save: < FRAMES.CHP>.

Here is how to use < FRAMES.CHP>. Before you start, use HOTSHOT's CVRT program to gray-scale the appropriate PCX files in your directory.

Step 1. Open Ventura and call up < FRAMES.CHP>. Select: **View, Facing Pages View.**

Step 2. Select: **File, Load Text/Picture, Image, PC-Paintbrush.**

Step 3. When the pop-up ITEM SELECTOR MENU appears, reset the Directory to C:\PICTURES*.PCX.

> **NOTE**: The next step will proceed much faster if you use Ventura's: **Options, Hide Pictures**. Otherwise, you will have to wait as each picture is displayed.

Step 4. Load one picture into each of the frames. On your screen you will see two pages at once (four frames), so the loading can be done very quickly. Refer to Figure 7–7.

Step 5. Select: **File, To Print, All.**

Get a cup of coffee while the pictures are printing. The length of your coffee break is determined by the number of pictures in the file. Number each image so that you can identify it. At this point, you have hardcopy images that can be pasted onto camera-ready page masters. You also have a (PICTURES) directory with images that can be inserted electronically into a document.

IMPORTING PICTURE FILES

Ventura handles line art in a number of different file formats, including: GEM, AutoCAD DXF, Lotus 1-2-3, Mentor Graphics, PICT, CGM, PostScript, and HPGL. Ventura also handles picture files in PCX or IMG format and files from GEM, Dr. Halo or MacPaint.

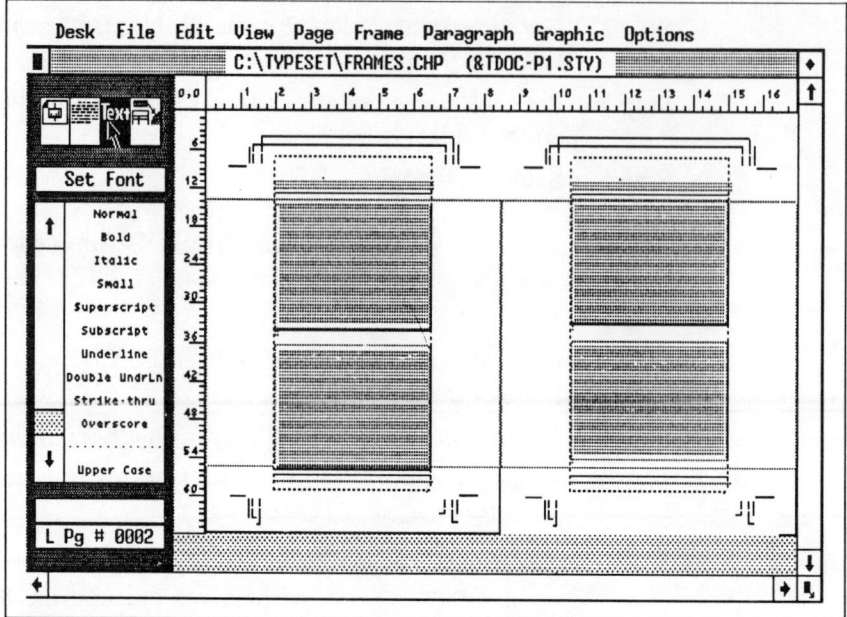

Figure 7–7. Ventura screen shows facing pages view of FRAMES.

DXF (AutoCAD Format) Files

If you want to use DXF (vector-based) files from a drafting program such as AutoCAD, you have several options:

- Save the image as an AutoCAD slide (SLD) file.
- Convert the image to HPGL format.
- Use Ventura's DXFTOGEM conversion utility.
- Use an intermediary paint program.

These options present certain complications, and you may not get exactly the image you started with. Parts of fill patterns may be incomplete, text may be converted to another font, parts of the drawing (such as shapes and mirrored images) may be missing, and circles may not be round. Refer to Figure 7–8.

One solution is to use a scanner to capture the plotted image. As an alternative, use HPGL file output from AutoCAD. Another solution is to paste up the plotted image onto the camera-ready masters.

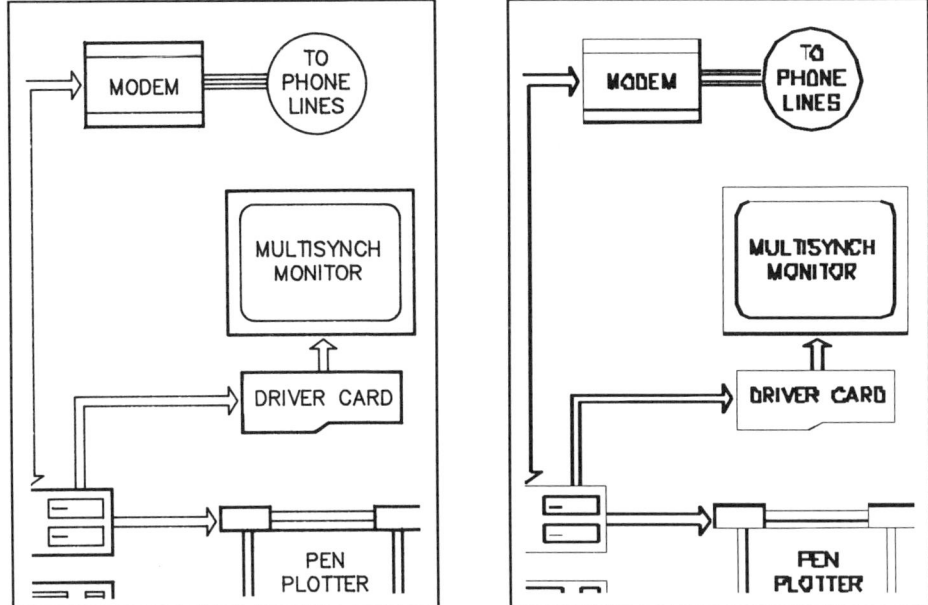

Figure 7–8. Imported AutoCAD images. (*left*) Plotted original; (*right*) AutoCAD SLD file.

Macintosh Paint and PICT Files

You will need a disk conversion utility, a network, or a modem to transfer picture files from a Macintosh environment into Ventura. Paint files always transfer as a full-size 8" × 10" page and PICT files may introduce complications. For example, bit images within PICT files do not convert and text fonts may convert to other fonts. The solution is to use a scanner to capture the plotted or laser-printed image into Ventura. Or you can paste up the laser-printed Macintosh images.

PCX and IMG Files

There is a graphics standard developing around the PCX file format. A number of paint programs, scanners, OCRs, and screen capture utilities use the PCX format. In addition, you can easily send PCX pictures via modem or network. Ventura converts all PCX files to IMG files. Files in PCX format are stored as a raster-based image. As the image is enlarged, the "jaggies" become more pronounced. To avoid this, size your images so that they will not need extensive enlargement. For the highest quality, start with a full-size image.

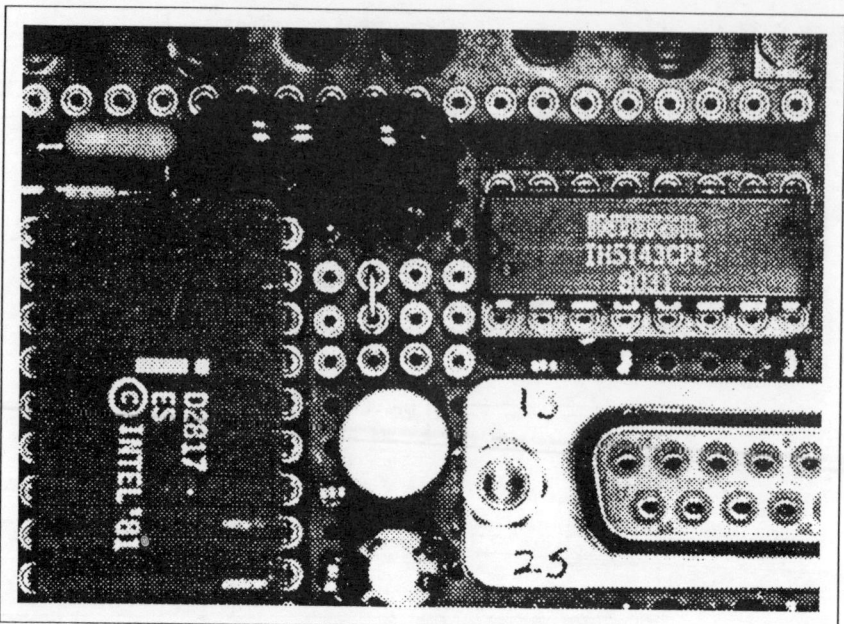

Figure 7–9. Scanned photo reproduced at 1:1 scale.

GETTING THE MOST FROM YOUR SCANNER

A scanner transfers photos, clip art, line art, and other 2-D images into your computer. All of the images in this section were generated using White Sciences' SCANGRAB software and a Canon IX-12 scanner. Figure 7–9 was scanned from a black and white photo.

The scanner's input can be either color or black and white photographs or any of various styles of line art. The next two figures show the effect of enlarging a raster-based image. Figure 7–10 is 25 percent larger than the original image and Figure 7–11 is twice the size of the original.

Although images are consistently produced at a resolution of 300 dpi, enlargements beyond the 25 percent level are impractical because the raster pattern or "jaggies" become objectionable.

Figure 7–12 was scanned from a sketch made with a purple felt-tip marking pen on inexpensive Xerography paper. The technical quality of the image approaches that of a charcoal or broad-pencil drawing on rough paper. You can experiment with colored marking pens and different photocopy machines or scanners. Machines from different manufacturers reproduce colors in different shades of gray.

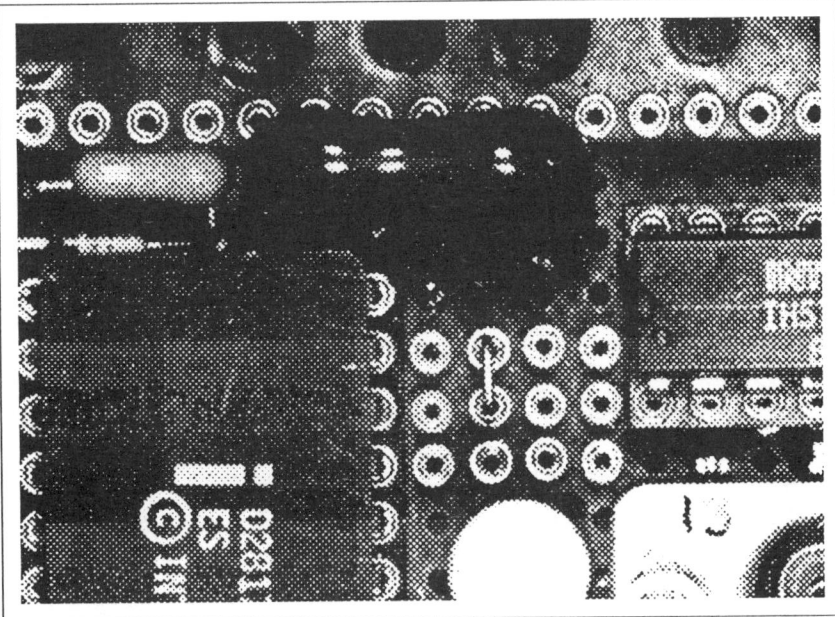

Figure 7–10. Scanned image enlarged 25 percent.

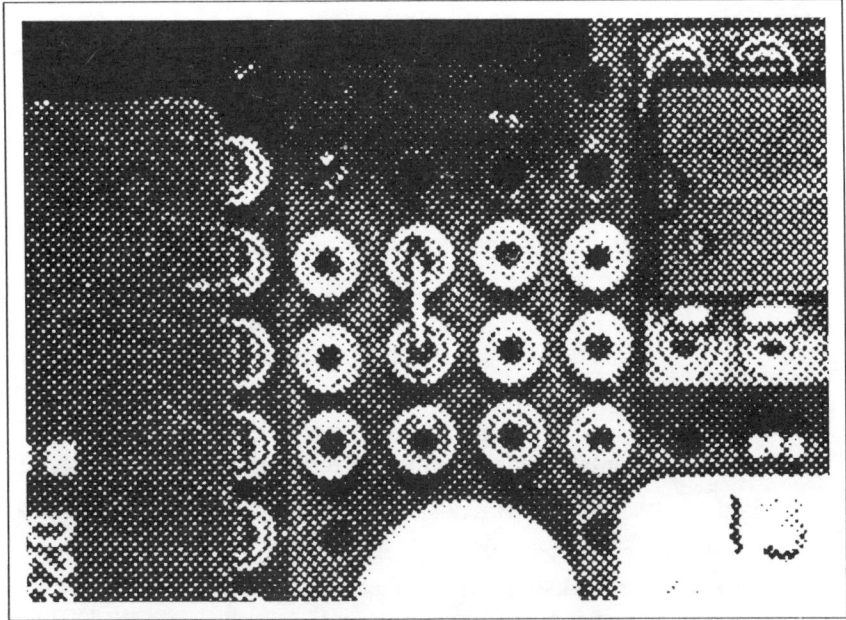

Figure 7–11. Scanned image enlarged 100 percent.

Figure 7–12. Scanned image from original sketch of Grubblie.

Using SCANGRAB

SCANGRAB is used from the C-prompt or from a separate (SCAN) directory. The program is designed to be used with a J-Laser or J-Laser Plus card at EGA screen resolution. To use the program, follow these steps:

Step 1.   Switch the scanner on. Insert the photo or drawing you want to scan.

Step 2.   At the C-prompt (or at SCANGRAB's directory) Type: SGRAB **ENTER**. In a few moments you will see the main screen. At the top of the screen are several menu items.

Step 3.   Use the arrow keys to move the highlight to the menu item of your choice. If you are scanning a photo, Select: **PHOTO**. If you are scanning a line drawing, Select: **LINE** and Press: **ENTER**.

Step 4.   (A pull-down menu appears with a choice of **LIGHT, MEDIUM** or **DARK**) Use the arrow keys to Select: **MEDIUM**.

Step 5.   The scanner starts automatically, and in a few moments, the scanned image appears on your monitor, together with the EDITING MENU.

Step 6.   Observe a square at the middle of the screen. This is the clipping window. Press: **NUM LOCK** (ON) and use the arrow keys to expand the window until it contains the area of the image you want to keep. Press: **NUM LOCK** (OFF) and use the arrow keys to move the clipping window without changing its size.

Step 7.   After you have clipped the image, Press: **ENTER**. The screen clears and the clipping window reappears (empty). Press: **ENTER** and the clipped image reappears within the window.

Step 8.   (At the screen menu) Use the arrow keys to Select: **OUTPUT**. In a few moments the clipped image is printed at your laser printer.

Step 9.   (At the screen menu) Use the arrow keys to Select: **SAVE** and Press: **ENTER**. You are prompted for a filename.

Step 10.   Type: EXAMPLE and Press: **ENTER**. The menu disappears as the file is SAVEd to disk.

Step 11.   (At the main menu) Select: **CLEAR**. The screen clears.

Step 12.   (At the main menu) Select: **DISK**. A pull-down menu displays all the stored picture files (with the file extension .MAT).

Step 13.   Use the arrow keys to Select: **EXAMPLE** and Press: **ENTER**. The clipped and saved image appears on the screen.

Step 14.   (To exit SCANGRAB) Press: **ESC**.

At this point you can use the <EXAMPLE.MAT> file in Ventura. Use the sequence: **File, Load Text/Picture, Image, PC-Paintbrush**. When the selection menu appears, change the directory (if necessary) and change the file extension from (.PCX) to (.MAT).

Precautions When Scanning

If you have a line drawing with vertical or horizontal lines, carefully align the original in the scanner so that the verticals/horizontals are parallel/perpendicular to the scanner. Otherwise you will introduce artificial "jaggies" into the image.

Use black ink for sketches and line art unless you want to produce special effects such as charcoal-like drawings that can be made with felt-tip marking pens.

Crop images to the smallest practical size. Each extra bit of unclipped area occupies additional storage space on your disk. As examples, the first picture in the scanner section of this chapter (Figure 7–9) occupies 96.4 Kbytes and each icon in Chapter 6 occupies 3.7–7.3 Kbytes.

Expect a slight reduction in quality and some increase in line thickness after scanning. As an example, Figure 7–13 shows an original pen plot (left) and the same image scanned and laser-printed (right).

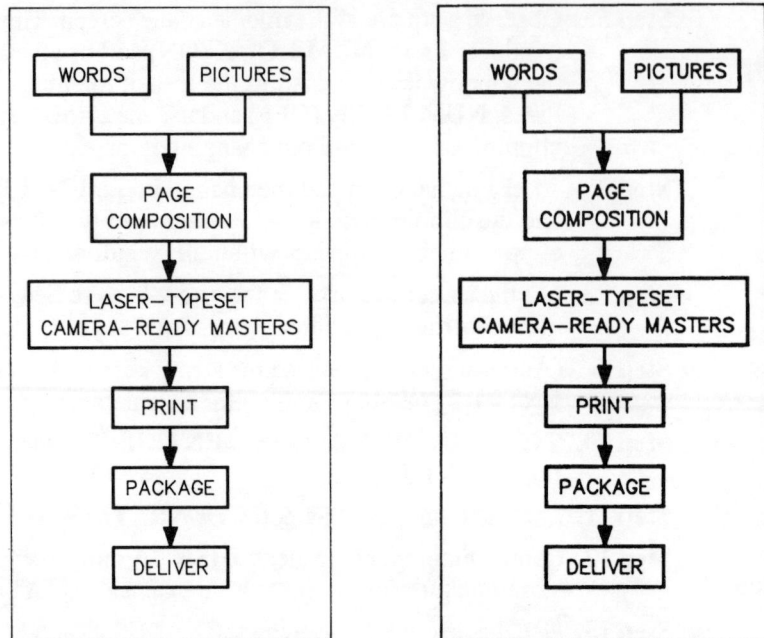

Figure 7–13. Pen plot vs. scanned and laser printed image.

LEARNING MORE ABOUT VENTURA

Nobody can teach you how to use Ventura or any program; it is something you will have to learn for yourself. There are guides, however, and once you have a working knowledge of the software, you will be ready for a Ventura tutorial, which can be found in the desktop publishing section of a technical bookstore or in some of the books listed in the Appendix.

ABOUT THE GRAPHICS IN THIS CHAPTER

Figure 7–1: Register marks were pasted up from a laser-printed page of "FRAMES" pictures. These register marks also appear on facing pages in Figure 7–7. The outermost register marks are 6" apart. The marks connected by horizontal bars are 5 ½" apart. The 5 ½" marks are offset to allow pages to be cut to size without offsetting the text on the screen. On the cut pages the inner margins are wider than the outer margins to accommodate holes for binding rings or a punch pattern for the wire binding.

Figures 7–2, 7–5, 7–6, 7–7: HOTSHOT was used to capture and gray-scale all of the screen images. The ruling box around each figure is 0.01" wide with a 0.10" space between the image and the ruling box.

Figures 7–3, 7–4: Text examples were handled within Ventura without pasteup.

Figure 7–8: The figure on the left is a pasted up pen plot. The figure on the right is an AutoCAD SLD file that was downloaded directly into Ventura.

Figures 7–9, 7–10, 7–11, 7–12: SCANGRAB was used to capture these images. The enlarged figures were made by changing the scale factors within Ventura. The ruling box around each figure is 0.01" wide with a 0.10" space between the image and the ruling box.

Figure 7–13: The figure on the left is an original pen plot which was then pasted up. The figure on the right was made by scanning the pen plot and capturing the image to disk via SCANGRAB. The image file was recalled within SCANGRAB, then laser-printed and pasted up.

Appendix A: Additional Information

This section contains recommendations for an affordable computer-aided-design (CAD) system and a description of the graphics in Chapters 1–4. For more information, refer to Chapter 6 and Selected Readings.

An Affordable CAD System

The following computer-aided graphics system produces line art suitable for publication. The system is slow but relatively inexpensive. Other hardware and software can be substituted for these items.

1. XT/AT computer with MS-DOS or PC-DOS, Version 3.0 or higher: 512 Kbytes of random access memory (640 Kbytes is better), a math coprocessor, two disk drives, or one disk drive and at least a 20 Mbyte hard disk.

2. Pointing device: A Logitech serial mouse for input.

3. Graphics adapter card and matching monitor: Although you can work with monochrome, color allows easier separation of layers (the equivalent of overlays). The graphics adapter card should produce a minimum of EGA resolution. For a few extra dollars you can have a VGA card and monitor.

4. Pen plotter capable of 0.001" resolution: Small plotters such as the Hewlett-Packard 7475A handle ANSI A-size (8 ½" × 11") or B-size (11" × 17") paper.

5. CAD software: From the dozens of software package that are available, two stand out: AutoCAD (over $2,000) and Prodesign II (about $300). Plan to spend about two weeks learning to use the software or training an operator.

About the Graphics in Chapters 1–4

Scheduling and project summaries in Chapter 1 are reductions of letter-quality printouts produced with MILESTONE software (Digital Marketing). Other drawings were prepared using AutoCAD software and a Houston Instrument DMP-61 plotter. Full-size drawings were plotted on vellum at a resolution of 0.001", using 0.35mm and 0.50mm liquid ink plotting pens.

Two computers were used to prepare the original text and graphics: a NOVA PC/XT computer (Computrade, San Jose, CA) with a 20-Mbyte hard disk, two 360-Kbyte floppy disk drives, and 640 Kbytes RAM; an AT&T 6300 (hard disk version) with a single floppy drive and 640 Kbytes RAM. Both machines are IBM compatible. The AT&T is faster and the NOVA has a larger card cage. Revisions to the original drawing files were made with AutoCAD, Version 10, running on a Compaq 386, Model 40, computer.

Appendix B: Producing This Book

Where's the Manual? began as a consultant's report that was written and published by Studio 7 in 1985-1986. At the time it was produced, this "typewriter manual" with plotted illustrations represented a cost-effective way to prepare a manual without desktop publishing tools. By 1988, affordable desktop publishing software and hardware were available and a supplement to the consultant's report was published. Some of the new text files were prepared with WordStar and others were keyboarded directly into Ventura as ASCII files. Additional line drawings were made with AutoCAD and plotted; screen images were captured with HOTSHOT, and SCANGRAB was used to reproduce the photographs. Both reports were printed in 8 ½× 11" format.

From the description above, it should be clear that the consultant's report and its supplement were produced using very different techniques and procedures. The editors at Van Nostrand Reinhold (VNR) suggested that Studio 7 might want to prepare the camera-ready masters for *Where's the Manual?*, because we had the electronic publishing tools in place; we were close to a number of excellent service bureaus, and we had been writing, illustrating, and preparing camera-ready masters for technical manuals for about ten years. In addition, all of the text was available as computer files and it made sense for us to do this. The VNR editors forwarded specifications and suggestions. We laid out a few sample pages and *Where's the Manual?* started to take shape. Figures B–1 and B–2 show samples of pages from the original reports.

MOVE can be executed the entity or image must be identified. This is accomplished by pointing (see POINT) or framing (see FRAME).

After identifying the entity or image, select MOVE from the screen menu. Reposition the cursor at the screen location to which the object will be moved. The object will follow the cursor. Press the left mouse button (or RETURN) to attach the object at the new location. The entity or image at the previous location will disappear.

ABC USER'S MANUAL

ERROR CODES

Throughout your instructions and examples, you've undoubtedly referred to Error Codes. Rather than describe or explain each Error Code in the instructions, put them in a table or list. The Error Codes are easy to find in this format. In defining Error Codes, three items are needed per entry:

- Error Code Identification
- Description
- Recovery Action

Error Code Listing

Short concise explanations are best. The objective is to provide your reader with a fast solution to a problem. Make your statements brief and to the point. Refer to the following example:

ABC USER'S MANUAL

ERROR CODE LIST

ERROR CODE	DESCRIPTION	RECOVERY ACTION
.....	.....	.....
.....	.....	.....
E-3	Swap file full	D
E-4	Disk full	B,G,H,I

Figure B–1. Sample page from original consultant's report (a "typewriter manual").

thing will be transferred at once. Remember to also copy the style sheet. Refer to the following example:

STEP 1 (At the C-prompt) Make a working directory called: WORK.

STEP 2 Load your word processing files into WORK. (For the rest of this example, we'll assume that one of your word processing files is named: INTRO.WS).

STEP 3 Start Ventura and select: **File, Open Chapter**. A pop-up menu appears with whatever working directory you were using last.

STEP 4 (At: **Directory**) Use < DEL > to remove the existing directory name. For example, if you were using the TYPESET directory, you'll start with: C:\TYPESET*.CHP. After you delete "TYPESET". You'll end up with: C:*.CHP.

STEP 5 Type: **WORK** < ENTER >. You'll end up with: C:\WORK*.CHP.

STEP 6 (At: **Selection**) Type the name of the first chapter of your manual. For example, type: **INTRO.CHP** < ENTER >. Refer to the following figure:

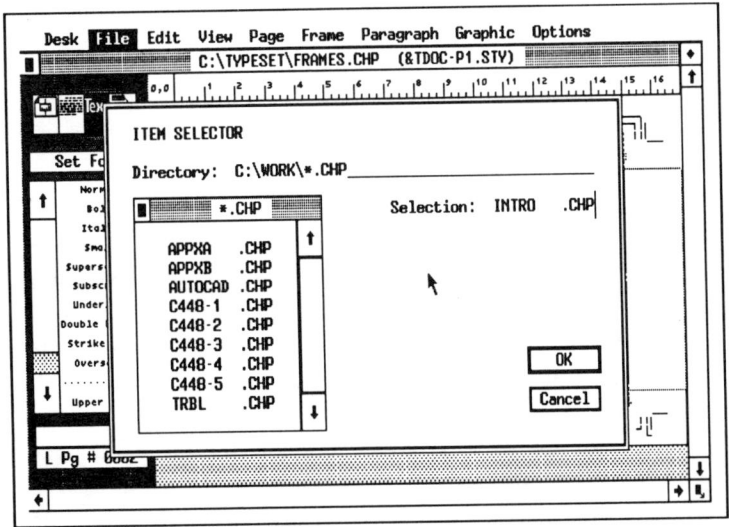

STEP 7 Select: **File, Load Text/Picture, Text, WordStar** (or whatever word processing program you're using) < ENTER >.

STEP 8 From the pop-up menu, select: **INTRO.WS** < ENTER >. Observe: The file loads and appears on the screen.

STEP 9 Rename your existing style sheet (for example): **ABC.STY.**

STEP 10 Use the: **File, Save As** option and at: **Selection**, Type: **INTRO.CHP** < ENTER >.

Figure B–2. Sample page from supplement to consultant's report.

DESIGN AND SYNTHESIS ISSUES

Although most of the material for *Where's the Manual?* had already been written, a major revision was needed to make the information current. Following the revision, VNR provided copy-editing and the corrections were incorporated into the manuscript. As we were making the corrections, a number of problems surfaced. Some of these issues are matters of perspective; however, most of these problems represent design and synthesis issues.

What We Say and What We Do

Often the format of a technical manual must be adjusted to correspond to the already-established style of a particular company or client. In the case of this book, the publishers have style and formatting guides that sometimes differ from what is recommended as good style and formatting for a software user's manual.

As one example, the use of contractions is recommended for a user's manual because the flow of words is akin to the way people speak and anything that serves to make the manual more friendly and conversational is considered a positive element. On the other hand, much literary writing, including books, newspapers, magazines, and corporate reports, is cast in a more formal style that usually avoids the use of contractions. So, it was not hard to understand why a professional copy editor would change "On the screen you'll see" to "On the screen you will see."

As another example, VNR and many other book publishers have guidelines governing the placement of figures on pages—they go at the top or at the bottom of a page. In a technical manual, the figure appears immediately after the first mention of it and, because of this, you will occasionally find blank spaces at the bottom of pages. There are other reasons for leaving blank spaces on pages in technical manuals but few of these are acceptable to book publishers. Book and magazine publishers, and also those editors who prepare corporate reports, prefer pages and columns that are equal in length, because such pages are aesthetically appealing and this format represents a more or less established practice among professional publishers.

Concerning the placement of figures and the blank spaces, a technical writer would argue that user's manuals are designed for easy revision. Often a package of "change pages" is sent out with *Remove and Replace Instructions* for various pages in the manual. Books, magazines, and corporate reports are not revised in the same way. If there are changes or revisions after a book is published, a new book is usually printed.

So, the publishers and the technical manual people have different ideas about things like contractions, figure placement, and blank spaces on pages—and both camps have valid reasons for their views. These issues crop up when one writes a book about preparing user's manuals. To resolve the conflicting ideas, *Where's the Manual?* follows the book publisher's guidelines and the examples that illustrate usage in a user's manual follow the technical writer's guidelines.

The Text Files

The tab settings in the text files of the original consultant's report presented a problem. WordStar utilizes two different tabs: the first is a standard ASCII tab and the second (which looks identical on the screen) is a tab consisting of a string of "space" characters. We had used both kinds of tab. With monospaced type such as that used in a "typewriter manual," there is no problem at all. With proportional type, however, a string of space characters expands or contracts along with all the other proportional characters, and text that appears to be vertically aligned in WordStar may be misaligned when transferred to Ventura.

We solved the tab problem by deleting all the strings of space characters. However, this was an impossible task with WordStar because strings of spaces and "real tabs" were indistinguishable on the screen. It is also a difficult task within Ventura because extra spaces are represented by short underscore characters and, at a resolution of 600 × 800 pixels, it is easy to delete a leading character along with the underscore marks.

An ASCII editing program called Brief was used to perform the deletions and to accomplish many of the other required corrections. Brief lacks some of the attributes of an excellent word processing program, however, it offers great flexibility and speed for editing. Here are some examples of the program's features: when used with a mouse, different macrofunctions can be called up and assigned to different mouse buttons; when the cursor is moved to the edge of the screen, the screen scrolls automatically; several windows can be opened on the screen and a different file can be displayed in each window; sections of text can be copied from one window to another; and the search and replace function is so fast that it seems to be immediate.

Spellchecking

Neither Brief nor Ventura has a spellchecking capability. A third-party program called VP-to-the-Max offers Ventura users not only spellchecking but also a search and replace function together with a dictionary and thesaurus—all of which can be used like any other menu option within the Ventura environment. VP-to-the-Max ignores the Ventura formatting commands (which appear in the text file). The thesaurus/dictionary provides synonyms, antonyms, and definitions of individual words. In the spellchecking mode, a misspelled (or unknown) word is flagged and a list of alternate words appears. You can choose the correct word from the list or make a new entry to the dictionary. VP-to-the-Max was used to spellcheck each chapter of *Where's the Manual?* and for many of the search-and-replace operations. The program is somewhat sluggish in operation, but its utility far outweighs the lack of speed.

Ventura's Professional Extension

The VNR editors were concerned about balanced page lengths and use of the correct typographical symbols for fractions and other equational expressions (e.g., ½ instead of 1/2). There were also specifications for tables that were difficult to execute with Ventura, Version 2.0. In order to provide these features, we used Ventura with the Professional Extension.

THE LASER PRINTING ISSUES

Studio 7's production facility is designed to prepare the camera-ready masters for technical manuals, brochures, and newsletters. For these purposes, a J-Laser card and a low-cost 300 × 300 dpi laser printer provides a cost-effective solution, and output that is two to five times faster than a comparable PostScript printing engine. However, it was clear that a resolution of 300 × 300 dpi was not acceptable for *Where's the Manual?*

In order to provide camera-ready masters at higher resolution it was necessary to create PostScript disk files that could be used by a service bureau. Although resolutions as high as 2540 × 2540 dpi are available with Linotronic laser typesetters, these services are expensive, the Linotronic uses special paper, and with an output rate of up to 10 minutes per page, it would take a long time to produce the camera-ready masters. We favored a plain-paper laser printer that was faster, and it seemed reasonable to accept a lower resolution.

Page Formatting and Width Tables

Fortunately, Ventura can be configured to produce direct output via the J-Laser card with a "plain vanilla" printing engine—and it also can be configured to produce a disk file usable with PostScript laser printers. The trick is to use a PostScript width table. The good news is that this trick enables you to print a PostScript-like file using the J-Laser hardware configuration and, when you do this, the line lengths, page lengths, headings, and other features appear as they will appear when the same file is printed on PostScript hardware. The bad news is that the individual text characters are not properly spaced because the J-Laser hardware expects to see a

Back Matter consists of reference material that is located at the end of the user's manual. Prepare this section before the Front Matter because it is more complex and contains vital information about the software. Refer to the outline in Chapter 1.

Back Matter consists of reference material that is located at the end of the user's manual. Prepare this section before the Front Matter because it is more complex and contains vital information about the software. Refer to the outline in Chapter 1.

Figure B–3. (*Top*) Text prepared with a PostScript width table and printed using J-Laser hardware and a QMS Kiss laser printer (non-PostScript) at 300 × 300 dpi. (*Bottom*) The same text prepared with a PostScript width table and printed on a QMS PS 810 Turbo laser printer (PostScript) at 300 × 300 dpi.

J-Laser width table and not a PostScript width table. With a J-Laser width table the letter spacing is different enough to produce different line lengths, and consequently text is placed from one page to the next differently from PostScript placement. Refer to Figure B–3.

In order to leave open all printing options, the page proofs for *Where's the Manual?* were prepared on J-Laser hardware with a PostScript width table—which did not particularly please the editor at VNR. The camera-ready masters were prepared on a NewGen PostScript printer at a resolution of 400 × 800 dpi.

Differences in Page Length

While experimenting with different laser printers, we discovered that the page length, measured from the top register marks to the bottom register marks, differs from printer to printer. The only practical solution to this problem is trial and error. To correct a similar problem, follow these steps:

Step 1. Use the Ventura **Frame/Sizing & Scaling** option to make a frame to your required page size.

Step 2. Place a ruling box around the frame.

Step 3. Print the page and measure the length and width of the ruling box.

Step 4.   Make the necessary adjustments.

Step 5.   When the ruling box is the exact size of your required page, use Ventura's **Graphics** option to construct the register marks.

Step 6.   Print the page again and measure between the register marks.

Step 7.   Delete the ruling box.

Square vs. Nonsquare Resolution

With "nonsquare" laser printers the thickness of thin vertical lines is different from the thickness of thin horizontal lines. Nonsquare printers are those printing at unequal vertical and horizontal resolution, for example, 300×600 dpi or 400×800 dpi. "Square" laser printers produce equal vertical and horizontal resolution, for example, 300×300 dpi or 400×400 dpi. Although a difference in vertical and horizontal resolution is relatively unimportant when printing text, this difference could be significant with line drawings. Figure B–4 shows enlargements of register marks produced on different laser printers.

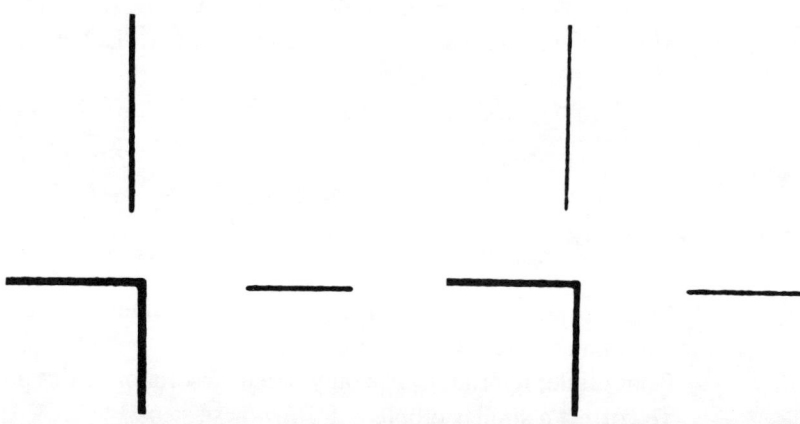

Figure B–4. Vertical and horizontal lines produced at different resolutions. (*Left*) 300×300 dpi, QMS PS 810 Turbo laser printer. (*Right*) 800×1200 dpi, Printware 720 IQ laser printer. Note that the intersecting lines are more equal in width. Also note that 300×300 dpi laser printers produce lines that are generally thicker than lines produced on printers of higher resolution.

Printing Resolution

Figures B–5 and B–6 show enlargements of parts of laser typeset pages at different printing resolutions. Both images are from plain paper laser printers that produce square output. To prepare these figures, the same text file was printed on each of the PostScript printers and the printed image was enlarged photostatically by 400 percent. The images were then pasted up.

Figures B–7 and B–8 show enlargements of parts of laser typeset pages at higher printing resolutions. Both images are from plain paper laser printers that produce nonsquare output. To prepare these figures, the same text file was printed on each of the PostScript printers and the printed image was enlarged photostatically by 400 percent. The images were then pasted up.

ront Matte

Figure B–5. 300 × 300 dpi, QMS PS 810 Turbo laser printer.

ront Matte

Figure B–6. 400 × 400 dpi, NewGen Turbo PS/480 laser printer.

ront Matte

Figure B–7. 400 × 800 dpi, NewGen Turbo PS/480 laser printer.

ront Matte

Figure B–8. 800 × 1200 dpi, Printware 720 IQ laser printer.

Glossary

Artwork. A black and white or color original prepared for reproduction.

ASCII. American Standard Code for Information Interchange. ASCII files contain only standard keyboard **characters**.

Binding. A term describing various methods for securing pages of a manual or book. Typical **binding** methods are loose-leaf, ring binding, saddle stitching, and perfect.

Bit-mapped. *See* **Raster-based**.

Body text. The ordinary running text in a document.

Bold (or **Boldface**). A heavy or thick version of a particular **typeface.**

CGA. Computer Graphics Adapter. A display format with a **resolution** of 350 **pixels** by 200 lines.

Chapter. In Ventura, a file containing pointers to text, graphics, a **style sheet**, and other files.

Character. An individual letter, number, or punctuation mark.

Crop. To cut a figure or illustration to fit a given area, or to remove unwanted background surrounding an image.

Digitize. To convert a line, position, or curve into computer-readable coordinates.

DPI. Dots Per Inch. A unit of **resolution** for laser, dot matrix, and electrostatic printers.

EGA. Enhanced Graphics Adapter. A display format with a **resolution** of 640 pixels by 350 lines.

Extension. The 3-**character** suffix after the dot in a filename. For example, in the filename < HARRY.DCR>, "DCR" is the file **extension**.

Font. A set of **characters** and punctuation marks in one **type style**. **Font** is used interchangeably with **typeface**.

Footer. A design element located at the bottom of each page in a document and containing information about the document.

Frame. In Ventura, a rectangle used to contain text or graphic **images**.

Halftone. An **image**, usually a photograph, which is represented by a pattern of dots.

Header. A design element located at the top of each page in a document and containing information about the document.

Image. A picture or graphic.

Indent. Space between the **margin** and the first **character** on a line of type.

Justification. Spacing of words and letters to create a line of specified length.

Kerning. Overhanging of certain **characters** to provide even spacing.

Layout. The arrangement of words and pictures on a page.

Leading. The space between lines of type. **Leading** is measured in **points**.

Line art. Illustrations without shading. For example, an ink-line drawing.

Lower case. Letters that are not capital letters.

Margin. The space between text and the edge of a page. There are four margins on each page: top, bottom, left, and right.

Modem. An electronic *black box* that conditions computer information for transmission to other computers or through telephone lines. **Modems** also condition incoming signals from other **modems** so the signals can be used by computers.

Multisynch. A multiple frequency device, usually an adapter card or a monitor, that can operate at several different **resolutions**.

OCR. Optical Character Reader. A device that scans printed **characters** and converts them into digital form that can be used by computers.

Pasteup. The manual operation of adhering illustrations, text, **register marks**, and other items onto a camera-ready master copy intended for printing.

Pen plotter. A mechanical drawing instrument that moves pens across drafting media and/or moves the media in response to computer-generated instructions.

Pica. A unit of typographical measure equal to 12 **points**.

Pixel. The smallest unit of a **raster-based image**, either on the screen or produced at a **raster** printing engine, such as a laser printer.

Point. The basic unit of typographic measurement. There are 72 **points** per inch.

Pointing Device. A mechanical or electro-optical machine that is used to move the cursor on a computer screen. Pointing devices often have switches or buttons that perform other functions. The mouse, digitizing tablet, joy stick, and trackball are examples.

Ragged. Lines of type that are aligned at one **margin** but not at the other. *Ragged right* describes lines of type that are aligned at the left side but not at the right.

Raster-based. Graphics software that defines shapes by assigning **pixels** on a display or output device. The resultant image is a checkerboard and when enlarged, the stairstepping or *jaggies* become obvious. *See also* **Vector-based**.

Register marks. Lines drawn outside of the *active area* which is inked and printed at the printing shop. **Register marks** are intended as a guide for aligning and cutting pages.

Resolution. The sharpness of an **image**. On computer monitors, **resolution** is expressed in **pixels**-by-lines (i.e., 640 × 350), on plotted drawings, it is expressed in thousandths of an inch, and on dot matrix, laser, and electrostatic printers, it is expressed in **DPI**.

Scanner. An electro-optical machine used to convert **images** on paper to digital **images** that can be processed by computers.

Select. Choose a MENU option.

Style sheet. A collection of information that describes the typographic **layout** of a page.

Tag. Formatting instructions for a Ventura paragraph. The **font, type size,** alignment, tab settings, and other information are all contained within a single **tag**.

Typeface. A unique design for a set of **characters**. Examples are Helvetica and Roman Times.

Type style. *See* **Font.**

Typography. The study of **type styles** and the art of arranging type.

Upper case. Capital letters.

Vector-based. Graphics software that defines points, lines, and vectors by coordinates and relationships. **Vector-based images** can be enlarged or reduced without degrading the quality of the **image**. *See also* **Raster-based.**

WYSIWYG. What You See Is What You Get. A term applied to page-composition programs featuring a screen display that accurately represents the page before printing.

Selected Readings

Books and Miscellanea

Cavuto, J. and J. Berst. *Inside Xerox Ventura Publisher (Third Edition)*. Ventana Press: Chapel Hill, NC, 1990.

Jantz, R. *Ventura Publisher for the IBM PC*. John Wiley & Sons: New York, NY, 1987.

Kleper, M. *The Illustrated Handbook of Desktop Publishing and Typesetting*. TAB Professional and Reference Books: Blue Ridge Summit, PA, 1987.

Miles, J. *Design for Desktop Publishing (A Guide to Layout and Typography on the Personal Computer)*. Chronicle Books: San Francisco, CA, 1987.

Nance, T. *Ventura Tips and Tricks (Second Edition)*. Peachpit Press: Berkeley, CA, 1989.

Seybold, J. and F. Presser. *Publishing From The Desktop*. Bantam Books, Inc.: New York, NY, 1987.

Ventura Publishes (newsletter). Ventura Publisher Users Group: Morgan Hill, CA.

Xerox Ventura Publisher Compatibility Guide. Xerox Corporation: Rochester, NY, 1988.

Electronic Publishing References

The following references are a guide to other sources of information. The list is intentionally short. Electronic publishing is a rapidly developing field and many references become outdated quickly. Items preceeded by a (*) are reports or magazines that should contain up-to-date information.

(*) *Computer Graphics World.* 1 Technology Park Dr., Westford, MA 01886

Kater, R. and D. Kater. *The Printed Word.* Microsoft Press, 1985.

Labuz, R. *How to Typeset from a Word Processor: An Interfacing Guide.* R.R. Bowker Co., 1984.

(*) *MicroPublishing Report.* 2004 Curtis Ave., Redondo Beach, CA 90278

(*) *Personal Publishing--The Magazine of Electronic Page Creation.* 549 Hawthorne Ave., Bartlett, IL 60103

Robertson, B. Page Making on Your Micro. (Special Report) *Popular Computing*, p. 60, November, 1985.

Seybold, J. *The World of Digital Typesetting.* Seybold Publications, 1985.

(*) *The Seybold Report on Publishing Systems.* P.O. Box 644, Media, PA 19063

Simonsen, R. Bring the Power of Publishing to Your PC. (Special Report) *Popular Computing*, p. 56, November, 1985.

(*) *Typeworld*-The Newspaper of Word Processing, Typesetting, and Graphic Communications. 15 Oakridge Cir., Wilmington, MA 01887

Related Articles by the Author

McGrath, R.,   Prodesign II, CAD on a Budget. *Computer Graphics World,* 8/12 (1985) p. 69.

McGrath, R.,   Logitech's Mighty Mouse. *Computer Graphics World*, 9/5 (1986) p. 113.

Affordable PC Publishing. *Computer Graphics World,* 10/3 (1987) p.113.

Capturing Screens. *Computer Graphics World,* 10/5 (1987) p. 103.

Paths to More Pixels. *Computer Graphics World,* 10/6 (1987) p. 101.

Desktop Publishing Revisited. *Computer Graphics World,* 10/9 (1987) p. 109.

Competing in the PC/2 World. *Computer Graphics World, 11*/2 (1988) p. 109.

Fast CAD. *Computer Graphics World*, 11/4 (1988) p. 105.

Versatile Plotting. *Computer Graphics World*, 11/5 (1988) p. 85

Index

About the Author and Studio 7

About the Author

Richard McGrath is the owner and Operations Manager of Studio 7 Technical Documentation (San Carlos, CA). Previously, McGrath was Manager of Product Publications for the Communications Group at Memorex in Santa Clara,CA, and before that a Sr. Technical Writer at Dalmo-Victor/Textron in Belmont, CA.

He received his B.S. from Tufts and M.S. and Ph.D. degrees at The University of Tennessee; he worked as a Sr. Research Scientist at the Oak Ridge National Laboratory in Oak Ridge, TN. McGrath has taught graduate-level radiation biology at the University of California, Berkeley, high school drafting at Sacred Heart High School in San Francisco, and technical writing at the University of California, Berkeley Extension. McGrath has written and published over 50 articles and books in the scientific and computer-electronics fields.

About Studio 7

Studio 7 Technical Documentation is a technical writing, graphics, and consulting business that specializes in user's manuals for computer/electronics hardware and software. The business has been in operation since 1980. When the business first started, Studio 7 produced "typewriter manuals" or prepared material that was then typeset for customers. As desktop publishing technology advanced, the in-house production equipment was updated to include faster computers with more memory, page composition software, and laser printing capabilities.

The main part of Studio 7's business comes from established companies and start-ups in need of quality service on short notice. Customers include advertising agencies, public relations firms, and publishers, as well as computer/electronics and software companies. Some examples are: Bricker & Evans Advertising; Calma Co.; Coats Wheel Balancer Corp.; Daisy Systems Corp.; Gray Strayton International; Logitech, Inc.; Mentor Graphics Corp.; Precision Image Corp.; Prentice-Hall, Inc.; and Seiko Instruments U.S.A., Inc.

Studio 7 produces camera-ready masters for user's manuals, brochures, newsletters, and books. For businesses with in-house writing or production departments, Studio 7 provides writing and writing management, critical reviews, consulting services, advertising copy, and marketing or promotional material. The Studio 7 business philosophy is straightforward: provide excellent documentation at competitive prices and solve the customer's problems. That philosophy is reflected in the content of this book.